THE ART OF LEADERSHIP

Compiled by Seema Giri
#1 International Best Selling
& Award-Winning Author

UPLYFT
Media

The Art of Leadership

Uplyft Media
5922 Rosewood Road
Dublin CA 94568.

ISBN 978-1-7350255-3-7

CONTENTS

Part 1: LEADERS IN ACTION

INTRODUCTION

Thank you for leaning into this powerful anthology. It is my honor and pleasure to bring forth to you amazing heart centered authors who have opened up their hearts to you. *Art of Leadership* is an excellent and powerful resource for you to help you break free from your challenges or barriers holding you back from becoming the leader that you truly are.

Each one of us needs encouragement and wisdom from someone who has walked in similar shoes before. There are some lessons that we need to learn ourselves, yet there are many lessons we can learn from others and save ourselves time and pain. I hope you find lessons you can learn from the lives of these co-authors.

This book is one to be read as the spirit moves you. What do you need to hear today? Do you need a story of courage, of pathos, of redemption? Choose a chapter and see what unfolds. You will find just what you need in the pages of this book.

It is divided in three sections:

Leaders in Action: here the co-authors share the ways you can be a dynamic leader.

Transformational Leaders: here the co-authors share their transformational journey of becoming the leaders they are today; they share the wisdom and insight during this process.

Authentic Leadership: here the co-authors share how you can fully embrace the whole you and create your unique leadership style.

The following are some tips and suggestions on how to get the most out of this book and experience transformation.

1. You will need your favorite journal, favorite pen and a quiet place where you won't get disturbed.

2. In your journal, you want to capture your current state: your fears, frustrations and where you feel you are holding yourself back or being held back. Be as detailed as you can. This is for your eyes only.

3. First read through *all* the chapters.

4. Go to the chapter you resonated with the most and follow the tips given in that chapter. Use your journal to capture your thoughts and feelings.

5. Go to the second chapter that you resonated with and follow the tips given in that chapter. Continue doing so with the other chapters until you feel complete.

6. Review your journal. Go back over the pages, and you will gain new awareness and a new perspective of your challenges. You will notice your strengths. Perhaps you will even notice a pattern. Once you have this new insight, you will know exactly where you need to make some changes or adjustments to your life. Most importantly, you will see how far you have come in your leadership journey.

As you go through this process, you will realize, as you move through your leadership journey, you will resonate with the different authors' stories and tips.

Don't forget to celebrate your small wins along with the big wins!

I believe that life is supposed to be joyous and vibrant. The journey can be made with ease and grace. You're a diamond waiting to be polished so that you can shine with the gift(s) you were given in this world. In other words, you can give meaning and purpose to your challenges so that you can live your dreams.

The best way I have been able to serve is by providing creative solutions to help people grow and thrive. Compiling stories of remarkable people who have overcome some of life's most difficult challenges and thriving is one of the ways. One story at a time, one book at a time.

Now it's your turn: will you lean in to take in all that you can to change the trajectory of your life from the wisdom that you gain from these pages?

MINDFUL LEADERSHIP

USE MENTAL RECOVERY BREAKS DURING YOUR WORKDAY TO BOOST PRODUCTIVITY AND REDUCE STRESS

DR. KATHERINE LARSON

"You're gonna want to take a running jump," the camp counselor casually stated with a wave of his hand. "Aim for the yellow or red stripes. The further out the better." I gazed down at the blimp bobbing to the ebb and flow of the lake and gulped in fear. Twelve-year-old me had mentally prepared to muster the courage to jump off the 10 ft platform and onto the floating blimp. However, nobody had mentioned anything about launching myself off the wooden edge from a running start! "Don't be scared," I said to myself. "You can do this!" "You will always wonder what you missed out on if you don't jump," I convinced myself. "You can do it!"

I knew that reaching the red and yellow stripes eight to ten feet in front of me seemed impossible. I also knew that the only way to get there was to go all in, to take a full-blown running leap of faith. And I knew that once I was in the air, there was no turning back. Gravity would carry me downwards until the weight of my body hit the air-filled vinyl and popped the kid waiting on the other end of the blimp up into the sky.

I stepped to the back end of the wooden platform. Then I took a deep breath in, focused intently on the red and yellow stripes, willed my shaking legs to run, and launched myself into the air. I landed on the yellow stripes of the blimp with my eyes bright and adrenaline pumping through my veins, elated that I took the risk and hit my target.

Stepping into leadership is like my first time jumping off the wooden platform and onto the blimp. Leadership is being willing to take the first leap into the unknown before anyone else. It's scary. It takes courage. And when you do finally take that leap, you will feel the rush of the wind in your ears and the weightlessness of your body surrounded by nothing but air. You won't be on the sidelines wondering what you missed out on because you didn't take the jump.

While stepping into leadership requires courage, sustainably balancing the demands of leadership with health, personal life, travel and other interests is another challenge altogether. A challenge that plagues any high achiever or professional working a fast-paced job. Mental fatigue, overwhelm, anxiety and stress run rampant in the day-to-day lives of working professionals. While many of us resort to blaming these feelings on external factors such as our jobs, a global pandemic, our co-workers, our age or not enough hours in the day, what if these external factors weren't what was holding us back? What if what was holding us back from leaving behind work fatigue, overwhelm, anxiety and stress was our approach to professional work altogether? Allow me to share a story with you from my life about what's possible.

"BEEP, BEEP, BEEP!" a blaring alarm shakes me awake. I blink my weary, sleep-drunk eyes open, crawl out from under the work desk, and crack open a fresh 100-page patent application. Lunch time was over.

I was just like you, tired, stressed and feeling like there was not enough time in the day. And I decided in that moment to make a change. It took me quitting my job, a month long trip to India, 400 hours of yoga trainings, over 400 hours of transformational leadership coaching, experimentation with reiki and other energy healing modalities, years of productivity research and countless hours of trial and error on myself to develop the simple practices and proprietary systems my business partner, Joaquin, and I offer at CozyMind today. At CozyMind, we have unlocked a way to give your mind recovery breaks during the workday so that your daily mental stress propels you forward instead of wearing you out. We have strategies to recover your mind like Olympic athletes recover their bodies so that you can consistently perform at your highest mental level all day long. You don't need to fly to India, spend hundreds of hours on trainings or quit your job to learn from my experiences. And let me tell you, once I implemented CozyMind's 4-part strategy in my life, the shift was dramatic.

Now, I listen to the "tweet, tweet, tweet" of birds outside my window. My eyes are vibrant and alive. I take 5-minute or 10-minute mindfulness breaks throughout the day. These breaks prevent any mid-day slumps in productivity or my energy. Most importantly, my stress level is such that **I feel like I am on vacation while at work.** I have supported my clients in accessing this feeling. And I believe that everyone can feel like they are on vacation at work. Let me show you how.

At CozyMind, we use a 4-part consciousness recovery strategy to support you with implementing mindfulness during your workday. The first key strategy is mastering your mental recovery mindset. Taking mindfulness recovery breaks for yourself at work is going to be counter-intuitive for most people. The traditional work-culture mentality is that time is money and time spent away from doing work is wasted time. Additionally, our minds have trouble conceptualizing that 1 minute, 5 minutes, or even 10 minutes of doing anything, let alone mindfulness, is enough time to restore our energy or our focus after an arduous task. I am here to tell you that taking intentional 1-minute to 10-minute bursts of time away from doing work will support you in accomplishing more during your workday. Further, these short bursts of time away from doing work are so critical to your workplace productivity that you should consider these short bursts of time practicing mindfulness exercises billable work time. Indeed, meditation at work increased productivity by 120% in one Detroit study. In a 2016 study on mindfulness in the workplace, participants had a 31% reduction in stress and a 28% increase in energy a year after implementing mindfulness practices for 8 weeks (https://journals.lww.com/joem/Fulltext/2016/03000/A_Web_Based_Mindfulness_Stress_Management_Program.6.aspx). Knowing this, you can see why implementing mindfulness practices in micro doses every day has been so effective for our clients. And the first actionable step you can take toward mastering your mental recovery mindset is to think of mental recovery time as billable work time. Indeed, with mental recovery time having such a significant impact on your energy and your stress during work, your mental recovery time gets to be considered billable work time because it is critical for your work productivity and success.

The second consciousness recovery strategy we teach at CozyMind is mastering timing. Specifically, we teach mastering the timing of when to implement your mental recovery breaks, how frequently you should implement them and how long your mental recovery breaks should last. All these timing factors vary based on the individual and the types of tasks they are dealing with at work. An actionable item you can start now to support with timing is to find your productivity sweet spots. To find your productivity sweet spots, make a log that tracks tasks by time of day, time that the task took you to complete and your energy level after the task was complete. You will find that you will be more efficient with specific tasks at certain times of the day. You will also find that different tasks require different amounts of energy from you. We recommend using longer mindfulness breaks after tasks that require more energy. We also recommend completing tasks at times of day where you are most efficient. Timing is HUGE for our clients. To give you an idea of the impact of our full-day intensives, our clients are less stressed after a full day of work than they were when they woke up that morning!

The final two key CozyMind strategies are mastering habit formation and mastering mindfulness practices. At CozyMind, eighty percent of the mindfulness practices we teach and recommend are either a form of breathwork (also referred to as pranayama) or a meditation. When starting out, breathwork practices are the easiest and most flexible (in terms of time) to implement. An easy breathing exercise you can do today is a box breath. This breathing technique is commonly used by Navy Seals to reduce anxiety and improve focus during missions. Box breathing is a 1:1:1:1 ratio of breath traditionally coached as breathing in for a count of four, holding the breath at the top for a count of four, exhaling for a count of four, holding the breath at the bottom for a count of four and repeating. You can find a free guided box breathing session on our Instagram@cozymind.me.

When it comes to mastering habit formation, it is all about mastering behavior. To do this, you will need to assess the motivations, actions and prompts that dictate your day-to-day behavior. To decrease a behavior, motivations and prompts will get to be lowered to reduce the likelihood of taking certain actions. To support a new behavior (a new action you'd like to take), you will get to boost the prompts for that action and the motivation around taking that action. If your motivation level isn't capable of being changed, evaluate whether the action gets to be modified or if you only need to boost your prompting. With the right combination of action, motivation and prompt, new habits are easy to create and habits that don't serve you are easy to let go of.

An actionable item you can start now to support with masting mindfulness and habit formation is to choose a single mindfulness practice to implement at a time. Often our egos want to implement multiple mindfulness practices at once to create "faster results." However, consistency is king when it comes to integrating mindfulness breaks into your work life. Indeed, when it comes to consistency slow is fast. Thus, stick with adding a single mindfulness practice into your work life at a time to create the fastest results.

Ultimately, our 4-part consciousness recovery strategy of mindset, timing, mindfulness and habit formation mastery will enable you to use mindfulness practices during the workday to create success without stress. However, implementing mindfulness breaks during your workday is counter intuitive. Thus, many of our clients reach out to us for professional support for themselves and their teams. To this end we offer our CozyMind intensives. CozyMind intensives are do-it-with-you programs that enable you to find mindfulness practices that effectively recover your mind. Our intensives also support you with creating habits so powerful that taking mental recovery breaks after tasks becomes as effortless as checking your watch for the time.

At CozyMind, we have unlocked a way to give your mind recovery breaks during the workday so that your daily mental stress propels you forward instead of wears you out. We have strategies to recover your mind like Olympic athletes recover their bodies so that you can consistently perform at your highest mental level all day long. I believe the traditional approach to work is broken and that by implementing mindfulness during your workday, everyone can feel the same stress level as being on a tropical getaway, even after a full day of work. I encourage you to work smarter not harder. Especially in a post-pandemic world, ways to mitigate stress are essential to our day-to-day professional success. So what are you waiting for? Take the action steps below to kick-start implementing mindfulness during your workday today!

How To Kick-Start Implementing Mindfulness During Your Workday

1) Think of mental recovery time as billable work time.

2) Find your productivity sweet spots.

3) Implement regular breaks at the beginnings and ends of work intervals.

4) Choose a single mindfulness practice to implement at a time.

Dr. Katherine Larson

As the CEO and co-founder of CozyMind, Dr. Katherine M. Larson (Dr. Kara) is a Mindfulness & Performance Expert, who specializes in workplace mindfulness, emotional intelligence and productivity.

Dr. Kara is a Doctor of Biomedical Engineering as well as a Yoga Alliance Certified Instructor. She holds additional certifications in Health Yoga Life Coaching and Functional Diagnostic Nutrition®. Dr. Kara has invested over 400 hours coaching over 100 professionals. As the CEO of CozyMind, she works with professionals to accelerate productivity and reduce stress by implementing simple mindfulness breaks at strategic points during their workday. Her mission is to shift the current work paradigm to enable success without stress for all working professionals.

Dr. Kara is an international traveler who can be found exploring 12th century Cuenca in Spain, eating spicy miso ramen in Sapporo, Japan or white water rafting in Rishikesh, India. After her travels, she enjoys cuddling with her fluffy Samoyed, Flynn, who is CozyMind's adorable mascot.

Email Address: **hello@cozymind.me**
Phone Number: +1 (401) 830-0076
Website: **cozymind.me**
LinkedIn Page: **https://www.linkedin.com/company/71667082**
IG: **@cozymind.me**

FIVE KEY AREAS TO SHIFT YOUR BUSINESS AND SUCCEED DURING THE UNCERTAIN TIMES

ELLE BALLARD

Starting in early spring 2020, the whole world started experiencing a worldwide pandemic. Some of us were saying, "Oh it will end shortly and we will be back to our normal lives by the end of March." From the moment of writing this, a year after, March 2021, we are still in a global pandemic, some countries are still closed, some US states are releasing restrictions, some are not. A lot of families lost their loved ones. A lot of businesses had to shift, pivot or close, and a lot of other businesses prospered. My husband's company grew despite of this situation. My business had to shift a little, but no matter what was happening in the world, my business still grew.

Let us talk about why Leadership is important during the critical and uncertain times such as these and how other companies can act to continue to stay in business and bring in profits. There are five key areas that I exercised as a business owner to grow my business and shift what was not working. These five areas include Mindset, Vision, Action, Self-Image and Self-Care.

Mindset

When hard times hit, our mindset gets bombarded with a lot of emotions, media messaging, social media messaging, and this affects our thoughts and feelings. This also creates a lot of noise in your head, fear and anxiety. It is vital to plug yourself into a different information flow, different energy through daily meditations, journaling, meditational yoga affirmations or other mental exercises you prefer. During the times of a global worry, turbulence and emotional upset we have to take charge of our thinking. In fact, we have to do it daily independently of the outside world but especially during the challenging times in business. Since the pandemic started, we stopped meeting physically, we stopped going to networking events, restaurants and all public places closed; we had to turn to virtual meetings and Zoom or Skype calls instead. That allowed more time for other things such as morning and evening meditations. I started doing exactly that. I have to admit, it was hard to do for me at the beginning since I am normally a very social person; I was missing social networking events. Once I started meditating, though, I realized I needed this time for myself, this quality quiet time. I started discovering myself more, and listening to my intuition more; the more I meditated the more ideas I started receiving because my mind was silent and it allowed for new, fresh ideas flowing in. Whatever your preferred method of keeping your mind right, use it consistently and see changes happen in your life.

Vision

The next one is vision. During the difficult times it is important to turn back to what your vision is for your life and for your business, to remind yourself why you started this business in the first place. Ask yourself—what is my vision? What is it that you truly want at the end of the day? The answer you receive might surprise you and it might give you new perspective and new insight. By doing this exercise you re-align yourself with your true purpose, you remind yourself what truly matters and you are thus able to continue going forward with new perspective based on this reminder. This was exactly what I asked myself—am I clear in my vision, am I clear on my mission, am I aligned with it no matter what is happening in the outside world? When you know you are on your vision and mission, you truly know it and you are not fearful of what is happening around you because you know you are on the right path. Your clear vision helps you form a clear path and faith to keep going.

Action

When difficult times hit it is sometimes hard to take action, to think clearly, especially when the whole world is in panic mode. Once you know that you are on the right track and you identify what your vision is, it is important to keep taking action no matter the external circumstances. Some businesses decided to pause because they felt they were lost or because of restrictions imposed on them (which I definitely understand); still some businesses decided to introduce new programs and keep on going. That is what I have done I in my businesses. I redefined our three core Pillars that we are doing everything around in our business. Once I had done that, I started introducing additional programs that are aligned with these 3 Pillars and that will benefit our members. As a result of this exercise, we introduced new digital programs such as bi-monthly Masterminds for members, Culture connect meetings, and Business Expos. All virtual programs. This created an enormous advantage and I learned that people welcomed these programs with such excitement, and we are still continuing with those and making them better and better. During this process, I also realized the importance of creating curated programs for our members; I have seen great results with that strategy.

Self-image

When we are working in building our business and attracting clients, people always buy who you are. Your brand is YOU. Your self-image is also your attitude towards situation, towards people. How do you welcome each day when you wake up? I am sure you heard the saying, "There is nothing good or bad but thinking makes it so" by Shakespeare. Whatever happens in our lives, we decide how to react to it, and that is our own perception of the situation. If you face the world with the attitude of gratitude and positivity, and connect to people from that energy and vibration, people will gravitate toward your brand and your message and your persona. People want to be with other people who lift them up. Your attitude is your self-image. If you want to reach your specific goals and become the person you want to be, start acting like that person. Your thoughts and feelings are part of your attitude, and that is why the exercises we talked about in the mindset section are so vital for achieving this. The other side of this also who you surround yourself with and books you read or information you receive daily; this also shapes your self-perception and self-image. I recommend keeping yourself informed but not at the sake of your mental peace and healthy attitude.

Self-care

While your mindset is so important and our thoughts control everything we do, our physical health, our appearance and our body have to match and reflect that. Your eating habits, your exercise regime, your sleep, your time off are so important for us to continue to thrive and build our businesses. Choose an exercise for your soul, something that makes you truly happy. I, for example, am not a fan of running or building bulky muscles. I want my body to be toned, and I want to do an exercise that makes my soul happy. Choose an exercise for you, whether it is yoga, running, treadmill, swimming, golfing, etc. My soul exercise is ballroom dancing. Unfortunately, I had to stop attending our dancing studio since the pandemic happened, but a small group of us started gathering online for dancing exercise in the kitchen at home, and then I found a YouTube channel that I could exercise with at home. Dancing gives me such joy; music warms my heart, makes me happy, makes me excited. Sometimes I take short breaks between my busy day and just dance. I also love dancing naked in the morning in front of the mirror; try it, it is amazing!! You feel a burst of energy, love and happiness. No matter how I feel, I know once I start dancing everything shifts. When you love the exercise, you do not notice the workout, time flies and you are not only getting a workout, but your soul gets a workout and inflow of amazing, happy energy. Find the exercise that makes you feel happy and do it consistently.

In conclusion, these five key areas combined when exercised consistently will give you more clarity, perspective and help you keep yourself on your goals. We have to keep working and upgrading consistently and always; the minute we stop, we shift back to our old thinking that does not help us. That is why these areas have to be consistent parts of your daily or weekly routine, especially during challenging times. I am thankful for this discovery for myself. Once I learned who I truly am and turned to my inner self, everything started to make sense, the right people started coming into my life, things started shifting for me and I truly felt aligned with what I am doing. At the same time, I was ready to let other things go that no longer made sense for me and my purpose.

Doing these exercises consistently will positively contribute to your overall goals, and you are then ready to meet any challenge you face, have the right attitude and let yourself grow through this experience.

Elle Ballard

I help multinational women become diversity-aligned, fulfilled, and happy leaders.

I built a successful career in marketing, helping companies promote their products nationally and internationally. Today, I am a certified Leadership Trainer, best-selling Author, and Speaker. I have been leading different kinds of teams starting in the International oil and gas pipeline project, continuing in the networking industry, and now expanding and growing Women of the World Network (WOTWN). I have been a featured guest on the following podcasts: Expand Your Fempire, The Art of Feminine Marketing, Voice of America, and others.

I am open-minded, conscious leader who is always striving to grow, overcome, and better myself while listening to my inner voice and trusting myself in the process. Having to start from point zero several times in my life, I know how challenging the transition can be while maintaining your authenticity and individuality - that is the reason for creating WOTWN.

I love authentic women–women of substance and I believe in developing a diversity-aligned and happy women leaders who then positively impact future generations.

I love coffee, beautiful views, ballroom dancing, and interested in longevity and holistic health.

Website: **https://www.elleballard.com/**
Instagram: **https://www.instagram.com/theelleballard/**
Facebook: **https://www.facebook.com/theelleballard/**

WOTWN website: **https://www.womenoftheworldnetwork.com/**
WOTWN IG: **https://www.instagram.com/womenoftheworldnetwork/**
WOTWN FB: **https://www.facebook.com/WomenOfTheWorldNetwork**

YOUR LEADERSHIP LEGACY *ONLINE*: 4 POWERFUL STEPS TO GROW YOUR BRAND AND CREATE YOUR LEGACY AS AN EXPERT AND THOUGHT LEADER

DIANA CONCOFF MORGAN, MA, HHE

Have you ever considered deleting your social media? When I was about 3, my brothers, 4 ½ and 6, used to chase me around the house. I would run as fast as my little legs could carry me. When I got tired, I would stop and lay down on the floor, face down and hide my eyes from them. They would stop chasing me so I thought they were gone. When I got up, they would pounce on me! ***Social Media is just like that! You can run but you can't hide!***

It's not that we don't like social media, it's that we don't like what people sometimes do with social media. Social media can be negative, superficial, ridiculous, even hurtful. ***And social media can be a powerful force for creating positive change in the world!***

"Every sweet hath its sour."
—Ralph Waldo Emerson

"Let's elevate the quality of social media in order to use social media to elevate humankind."
—Diana Concoff Morgan, MA, HHE

"Knowledge is Power."
—Thomas Jefferson

My goal is to inspire you to elevate your message on social media to grow your brand and legacy as an expert and Thought Leader. My hope is that you will start embracing social media, actually enjoy it, share your message and create the healing and transformation you bring to the world as an expert and Thought Leader and gain new clients if that is your intention.

What Is Your Legacy Online?

What do you want people to remember about you, your message, your mission, your movement, online and offline? Your Thought Leader Legacy is about you as a person and your mission! It's also about your business.

Think about your brand. What do you want people to experience when they land on your website, your social media platforms or when they see your message in their social media newsfeeds?

Intentional Social Media

We are all Thought Leaders in different ways in our lives! Some of us have more followers than others. You're making an impact with everything you do on the internet, including your social media, so be intentional. You are creating a lasting brand online. Every action you take on the internet leaves a digital footprint. Consider the path of your digital footprint with every step you take. Show up as the Thought Leader that you are through what you "LIKE," comment on and share, who you follow, connect with, "friend" and interact with. It all shows and your followers are watching you. **This is a very powerful way to elevate your leadership brand and reputation online and create a lasting legacy of who you truly are.**

My Why

I've always been on a mission to inspire people to have a voice, share their message, be heard and seen. That has been my purpose, ever since I emerged from feeling powerless, silenced, invisible as a child. Once I found my voice, I never lost my passion for giving that gift to others!

Trained as a teacher, in my early 20s, I was seduced away from teaching by a short-lived corporate career. I didn't fit in the corporate culture, once again feeling silenced. It wasn't my path or my world. When I became a mom, I was changed forever. My son came home from school one day complaining that he hated school. That was the turning point.

I decided to create a business out of my true passion. I went back to school, got my MA in Holistic Health Education and Counseling and became a certified coach and an ordained Non-denominational Minister. In 1990 Blessings To You Wedding Ministry was officially launched. I loved it because I got to give couples a voice, the opportunity to express their vision of their spirituality through their wedding ceremony! For the next 20 years I got to be a stay at home and a working mom, officiate over 1000+ weddings, train and coach many other officiants to do this work and coach hundreds of couples to deepen their relationships. I also got to participate in starting a charter school and teaching Spanish. Most importantly, I got to be present as a mom. Today I know in every fiber of my being that my presence made a difference, both as a mom and as an entrepreneur!

I attribute my entrepreneurial success at that time to three factors: my passion and ability to create sacred space and foster heart connections, my knowledge and experience as an entrepreneur and mastering internet marketing. In the last 10 years of that business, I learned it all: websites, search engine optimization, blogging and eventually social media. Twenty years into that business, I began to explore my next adventure. How would my gifts, talents and skills best serve my purpose of facilitating giving others a voice, bringing healing to the world?

I became passionate about supporting purpose driven women and men who were healing the world with their lives, causes and businesses. The birth of social media created all kinds of new opportunities for healing and transformation in the world. And of course, it created obstacles as well. Now we had to be really visible, no more hiding behind our website and blog. The truth is, I was struggling to be seen and heard. All those childhood experiences of feeling powerless, silenced and invisible were offering me the opportunity for a huge healing! ***I remember the day I realized I was "the best kept secret with all my gifts and talents!" It was the day I stepped into my truth as a Thought Leader! This process resulted in the Whole Heart Social Media Success Formula.***

"Change happens when the pain of staying the same is greater than the pain of change."
—Tony Robbins

I had mastered the art of online visibility and client attraction. I was supporting other Thought Leaders and Changemakers when I realized I could help so many more people, make a much bigger impact if I became more visible myself. No more hiding! I had to move past my own fears, shyness and comfort zone that was behind the scenes! It was time for me to become visible! In doing that for myself, I have inspired so many others to do the same!!

The Whole Heart Path to Internet Marketing Success

The Internet is the great equalizer; anyone can become successful if you know what you're doing. It's a 24/7 network, just like any other networking event you attend, only virtual and never-ending. The truth is you can look like you're doing everything right and not be reaching the people you want to reach. Just because someone else is doing something on their social media does not mean it's the right action for you.

The Whole Heart Path to internet marketing success is for Thought Leaders and Changemakers. Setting yourself up for success takes more than just posting on social media and it's not something that happens overnight. It requires a strategy and it takes time and effort but the results are SO worth it! When you apply these strategies, you attract the people who are your ideal clients and referral partners and you create a legacy online that you can feel good about no matter who finds you anywhere on the internet.

These are the 4 steps to create your legacy online as a Thought Leader to powerfully master the internet to grow your mission, your movement and your business.

Step One

"Don't get caught chasing the Flash Mob."

Set Yourself up for Maximum Success

Create your own container for your legacy online. This includes your website, a blog and email marketing. Not everyone is ready for you right now. Email marketing helps you stay in touch with people until they are ready for you. You get to continue to educate, inspire and motivate them and build the relationships. Social media is a great marketing tool, but you can't rely on it always being there or always being the same. **There will**

always be a new place to "hang your virtual shingle!" If you don't have your own website and email marketing list, using social media is like chasing a flash mob, from one social media platform to the next!

Step Two

"Elevate your message to ensure your Legacy as a Thought Leader on social media."

Create a Clear Message That Reflects Your Brand

Your Thought Leadership Legacy is about how you want to uplift, inspire and transform the world. How do you want to use this very powerful tool, the internet, for positive transformation in the world? What causes are you passionate about? What inspires you? These are great opportunities to uplift and inspire through your social media.

Who Are You Talking To?

Every time you log onto your social media, start by asking yourself:

Who am I talking to? Who is my ideal client? What do I want to share that will inspire my ideal clients to "lean in?" You want them to say, "Tell me more." "He/she gets me." The internet is full of search engines. **Your success will always depend upon your clear message expressed with the right words, the words your ideal clients and followers would use to search for you!**

What Is the Struggle?

The more you are able to articulate the struggle that your clients experience, the more they will trust you and believe that you understand them. What is the struggle they express and what is the struggle you know is beneath the struggle they express? Give words to their unspoken pain and challenges.

What Is the Transformation?

What is the healing? What is the hope? There are many different levels of transformation. Share all of them.

Step Three

"Bring your Whole Heart Essence to your online presence."

You Are Your Best Lead Magnet

Everything is energy. The goal of your intentional internet marketing is for your ideal clients to experience the essence of who you are and what you do, visually, verbally, energetically as close as possible to what they would experience if they met you in person. Whole Heart Marketing is bringing your *whole heart*, your energy, your essence to your online presence to attract your ideal clients so people feel YOUR *whole heart*. This is how you stand out, shine as The Expert and Thought Leader you are and get noticed. This is the most powerful use of your time on social media. Because consciously or unconsciously, people feel your energy.

Step Four

"The Whole Heart Social Media Success Formula 50-40-10"

Create and Implement a Strategic Plan

Over many years and hundreds of clients I have developed a tried and tested success formula for Thought Leaders and Changemakers.

50% Brand Yourself

50% of your time on social media is for branding yourself. On your personal social media share your passion for your business. On your business social media, share your business. For many purpose driven entrepreneurs and Thought Leaders, the personal and business message are very intertwined. Branding yourself is being authentic, engaging, taking the time to connect, build relationships and share your message.

Here what that might look like:

CHALLENGE #1:

When you log onto your social media what's the first thing you think?

"What should I say?" From this day forward, I challenge you to make the 1 Degree Shift. Ask a different question:

"Who am I talking to?

What is their struggle?

What is the transformation?"

Be present twice a day, not just to share your message but to join in the conversation. Your authentic, *whole heart* personal interactions will attract more people than your own posts. Share other people's content as much as your own!

CHALLENGE #2:

What would it look like to *Bring Your Whole Heart Essence to Your Online Presence?*

Find 5 new people per week to start playing with. Here are some suggestions about who to "play with" on social media.

1. Find people who are active.

2. Make sure their message is in alignment with your message. (If not, you won't want to share their content.)

3. Find strategic partners, people who are marketing to the same or a similar group of people and selling something different. Or maybe they sell something similar and you can refer each other.

4. Play with other Experts, Thought Leaders, Changemakers and Industry Leaders.

5. Active networkers make great social media partners as well.

6. Connect with them on ALL of your social media platforms.

How to Play

Go to their social media platforms, personal and business. Get to know them.

"LIKE", comment on, share and **CARE**:

Connect with them.

Acknowledge them.

Respond to their comments.

Engage with them.

40% Position Yourself As the Expert and Thought Leader

"Marketing is inspiring people to take action on the thing you know they need."

40% of your social media activities are to educate, inspire and motivate.

Get people to share YOUR content into THEIR social media by sharing engaging, relevant, compelling content! Share on both your personal and business social media. Share personal inspiration and motivation on the personal social media. Share your business on your business social media. When you share about your business, focus more on the transformation, ***why*** it's important and not so much on the **"how to"** because that's what you sell! Share quality content that reflects your brand and core message, articles, quotes, images, videos, other people's content, always with your ideal client in mind.

10% Make Your Offer

10% of your online presence is promoting. Share something that's FREE so people can get to know you!!! Share this on your business pages, with an occasional post on your personal social media.

Conclusion

I hope I have inspired you to take the risk to step out, start showing up online even more, as your most authentic self to shine as a Thought Leader!! There are six degrees or less of separation between all people. We are, at most, six social connections away from anyone. In person, the connection is the handshake or a hug. On the internet, it's a hyperlink. Every minute, millions of "internet handshakes" occur. These are opportunities for you to build influence, network, connect, share your heart, your essence, your message, your mission, your movement and create the positive change you bring to this world!

Chapter Review:

The Whole Heart Path to Creating Your Thought Leader Legacy Online

Step One

Don't get caught chasing the Flash Mob.

Step Two

Elevate your message to ensure your Legacy as a Thought Leader on social media.

Step Three

Bring your Whole Heart essence to your online presence.

Step 4

The Whole Heart Social Media Success Formula 50-40-10

50% Brand Yourself

40% Position Yourself as the Expert and Thought Leader in Your Field

10% Make Your Offer

Conclusion

Show up and Shine as the Thought Leader that you are! Share your heart, your essence, your message, your mission, your movement and create the positive change you bring to this world!

Diana Concoff Morgan

Diana Concoff Morgan, MA, HHE, Marketing Strategist, published author, international speaker is a successful serial entrepreneur with over 35 years of experience including building 2 successful businesses using the strategies that she teaches her clients.

The mission of Whole Heart Marketing is to empower and educate Thought Leaders and Changemakers, including speakers, coaches, authors, holistic practitioners, healers and other entrepreneurs on a mission on how to master internet technology to:

Leverage the power of the internet to grow a sustainable business and life;

Cultivate increased Communication, Connection and Community among all people, everywhere;

Create your Brand and Legacy online so you can Shine as an Expert and Thought Leader;

Bridge the inter-generational gap that has been created by technology.

The Whole Heart Marketing Strategy is designed to increase connections and convert them into referrals and clients with tried and tested strategies. Diana has passionately helped hundreds of entrepreneurs grow their businesses, specializing in training on how to Master the Art of Online Communication, Networking and Client Attraction. She brings to her clients 35 years of experience including business development, sales, marketing, advertising, internet marketing, website development, SEO, blogging and social media, communication mastery, coaching and spirituality.

She understands the challenges of building a strategic and authentic online presence that will reflect your *whole heart* message, create your Thought Leader legacy online and bring you the right clients ongoing and has the patience and know-how to help you. Whole Heart Marketing offers a variety of strategic consulting services, coaching programs, and live virtual training and self-paced courses.

Diana@wholeheartmarketing.com
925-980-9052
www.WholeHeartMarketing.com
https://www.facebook.com/WholeHeartMarketing
https://www.linkedin.com/in/dianaconcoffmorgan/
https://twitter.com/dianarcmorgan
https://www.youtube.com/dianaconcoffmorgan
https://www.instagram.com/dianaconcoffmorgan
https://www.pinterest.com/dianacmorgan/

CREATE YOUR LEADERSHIP ROADMAP FOR MASSIVE BUSINESS SUCCESS

KELLY LOYD

"'Would you tell me, please, which way I
ought to go from here?' said Alice.
'That depends a good deal on where you want to get to,' said the Cat.
'I don't much care where—' said Alice.
'Then it doesn't matter which way you go,' said the Cat."
—Lewis Carroll, Alice's Adventures in Wonderland

My practice focuses on small businesses and entrepreneurs, and I often find that while those businesses are experts at what they do, like Alice, they don't have a clear idea of where they want to go. Oftentimes, they may not even know how much money they would like to earn, though they may have a vague idea of what they need to keep the business running and the lights on. Don't get me wrong, they are experts at their core enterprise - they just were never taught how to thrive at business, a totally different skill set.

Once they know where they're going, then we start the process of figuring out the "directions," or the plan that will help them achieve their vision. By doing this they (and their teams) find clarity and purpose, and understand the strategic direction of the company. **This is what leadership is all about**: creating a shared vision that will build a strong business with an eye toward the future.

Why is this important? Measuring milestones will help make sure that your business is really working for *you*, not that you are working for the business. You can use your business plan to create the lifestyle you want, whether you want to work 100 hours a week, or you want to work 20 hours a week. You can take a vacation or a sick day without feeling a cold lump in your stomach. You can have joy in your life, and your business will support your dreams.

I have been a goal-setter my entire life. When I was sixteen I decided that I wanted to buy a house. A lofty goal, but by the time I was eighteen I bought my first house, a two-bedroom, one-bath house in San Mateo, California. I just looked up that house on Zillow and my little starter home is now valued at $1.2 million dollars!

Owning my own home was ***real***. Simply put, it means security to me, for myself and my loved ones. I have probably never had such a compelling vision in my entire life. Because of that motivation I decided to buy a home again in 1999. I was a single mother and had been working two jobs for most of my adult life. Rent ate up most of my paychecks, and although I had a good job, I could never get ahead. The first decision I had to make was that while I would keep my job, I needed to relocate a couple of hours away and commute to work each day so that I could save up some money. That was a commute of four to six hours a day, on top of an eight-to-ten-hour workday. I won't go into detail about each of the steps I took to make that dream a reality, but there were several and they were major. However, the happy ending is that I was able to purchase a house again, and to add the sprinkles on the top of the cake, totally by a fluke of serendipity, I was able to purchase the house my grandparents bought back in 1907, and that my mother grew up in. It had been sold out of the family back in the 1960s and was on the market at the same time I was looking. The satisfaction I had in purchasing my home is immeasurable. The comfort I have in knowing that I can pass that house down to my son is indescribable.

That goal was personal, and it was hard. And it was a stretch. It was uncomfortable. And there were many pitfalls that had to be overcome. But I did it. And you can achieve your own goals too.

Choosing to own your own business is undoubtedly a stretch. Many of my clients leave jobs with a guaranteed paycheck and benefits for the uncertain future of owning their own businesses. And none of them would willingly go back to corporate life. To make sure that they never have to make that choice again, we work to make their dreams come true.

Below is an outline of the process my clients go through to set their goals. It is not all-encompassing. These are only the highlights of the process. Prepare for this goal setting process to take a full week, of an hour or two each day. It is intense, but it is important to go to this depth to create a true, workable guide for the next three months that will change "business as usual" to "business beyond your expectations."

The first part of goal setting is to create your Vision. This is your overarching vision of where you want to be in 5 or more years. Many people do this with a vision board. Or you might want to just write your vision in a notebook. Be sure to be as descriptive as possible. Be sure to note how much income you are earning, how many hours you will be working, whether you are taking a vacation, etc. Do your kids attend a private school or have college tuition? Do you own a home or rent? Do you have substantial retirement savings? Do you drive a different car than the one you own today? What does your office look like? Do you have a team? Do you work out of your home office or rent a space? All of these sorts of questions and their answers flesh out what you envision for your business and how it can support you.

The next part of goal setting is to look at your present state. If your Vision is to live in a waterfront property in Malibu in five years, while your present state is a business that is barely paying its way, you have a lot of heavy lifting to do. You may need to modify your Vision, or you may need to hone in on what will make your business a juggernaut that can support that lifestyle.

At the same time I had the goal of buying a house I also thought it would be really nice to get a car. Not unreasonable for a sixteen-year-old. The car I decided best suited my image of myself was a navy blue Rolls Royce. Hmmm. Later I decided that the car I really would like was a 1957 Corvette convertible. Both great motor cars, but I have never purchased either of them. Why? Because owning those cars was a fantasy—a dream—not a goal. I never put any effort into getting either one. I didn't create a plan or figure out the action steps I would need to take to own such a vehicle, including the maintenance and insurance. I have been satisfied with my little model Corvette that sits on a shelf in my office. I never felt a compelling desire to have the real thing. Make sure that your Vision includes those things that are real and compelling, but those things, like my fantasy cars, can be left in the "nice to have" category.

After setting a Vision that amplifies your desires for what you want in your life you will now drill down to what you can accomplish in three years, and then to what you can accomplish in this year. In other words, you are creating the map.

"Most people overestimate what they can do in one year,
and underestimate what they can do in ten years."
—Attributed to Bill Gates

Finally, with your current year in mind, decide on the one or two things that will get you closest to achieving your Vision in the next three months. That's right, one or two things. And only three months. One calendar quarter. Yes, there might be more that needs to be accomplished, but these one or two items will be the most important and the things that will propel your success. Bill Gates is right. Most of us try to accomplish too many things in too short a time period. But by remaining focused on the most essential things you can make tremendous progress.

Once you have determined these one or two things the real heavy lifting begins. Take each of those goals and break them down into action steps. You can do this on a blank wall with a large pack of sticky notes. Start writing down each of the steps you can think of and arrange them and rearrange them as you think of more actions that you will need to take. Create the chronological order in which these steps will take place. Once you have done this exercise—and it may take a couple of days to do, adding items and then letting them sit, then reviewing them again—transfer the action steps to your calendar.

If you are like most of my clients you will realize that while a lot can happen in three months, your goal may have so many action steps that you simply don't have time to accomplish everything in that amount of time. This is when you begin to figure out what steps you can delegate, simplify, or possibly eliminate and still achieve the results you want. Then you decide if there are personal sacrifices you need to make to be successful, and finally you review to see if your goal needs to be "right-sized" to be accomplished in the amount of time available. Remember, this is only for three months. You will be setting another goal at the end of this quarter, so don't despair. Often the goals set in the first quarter of using this system are setting the foundation for making massive progress in the ensuing months.

The next step after calendaring your progress is to have a daily review of your accomplishments, and weekly accountability. I will tell you right now that without the accountability portion, the likelihood of completing your goals drops dramatically. Make it a priority to join an accountability group or find a partner with whom you can hold each other accountable. If you are a business owner with a team, schedule weekly team meetings to go over each person's accomplishments and determine where they might need support to stay on target.

Finally, celebrate success at the end of each quarter. You set goals, aligned your team for success and may have worked with more purpose than ever. By focusing on just one or two key projects for an intense period of time you will have made great progress. You can now build on that success next quarter and every quarter thereafter!

Goals are the bedrock of successful leadership. Goals are strategy turned into action. And goals build a common purpose for yourself and your team. By setting just one or two focused goals at the beginning of each quarter you can create the business and lifestyle of your dreams.

Part of my practice is to help small business owners learn how to run their businesses like a business—using the same types of information that CEOs use when making decisions about the direction of the major corporations that we are all familiar with, but with tools that are geared toward the needs of entrepreneurs. My business is called Informed CEO for that very reason. Each small business owner is the CEO of their own company. We want you to be an *informed* CEO. We answer these questions together and my clients build the confidence and the business savvy to tackle any challenges that occur.

Kelly Loyd

Kelly Loyd is the business development expert that every small business wanted but couldn't afford until now. She has advised major corporations, local governments, and small businesses for over 25 years and is now bringing that expertise to small businesses like yours and your audience.

Kelly is the creator of InformedCEO.com, and is dedicated to advancing entrepreneurs and small business owners. Her high-impact speeches and seminars have empowered small business owners and entrepreneurs to learn the secrets of growth, profitability and goal-setting, just like the major corporations she once served.

kelly.loyd@informedceo.com
1-707-567-4113
https://www.informedceo.com
Facebook:
https://www.facebook.com/groups/informedbusinessbuilders
LinkedIn: **https://www.linkedin.com/company/67077074/**
YouTube:
https://www.youtube.com/channel/UCI-JWq0NPQue1pJwtTmbWUw
(Be Informed)
Instagram: **https://www.instagram.com/informedceo/Social media**

FOUR KEYS TO LEADING CONFIDENTLY IN ANY SEASON

SEEMA GIRI

The landscape of leadership has changed drastically over the course of the last two years. Change has always been difficult for humans to accept. Intuitively, we know that change is the only constant thing in life. Even so, it typically takes us a long time to move from tolerating it to truly embracing it. We fight against change and the inevitable adjustments it will make to our daily priorities and routines. The last two years have reformed all those tendencies. In part because we had no choice. The pandemic presented us with a heavy dose of challenge, difficulty and heartbreak. But, on the positive side of things, it has also given us the opportunity to realize that we can adapt very quickly and even embrace drastic changes when the need arises. We can pivot, making room for innovation to happen almost at the speed of light.

Often the most creative ideas for how to execute a fresh way of doing something will come during these crisis times when we are forced to look at a challenge with a new set of eyes. You might be surprised at the ingenuity and creativity that will bubble to the surface in your mind's eye as you seek novel ways to approach so much of your life and your work. You may have even discovered some hidden talents or a deep well of endurance that you didn't even know you had as you sought ways to hang on and even thrive during this pandemic. One thing for sure is those who have been adaptable and flexible have been able to shift, recreating the path of your plan that led you to success.

Being an entrepreneur, it might feel like you are living in a perpetual VUCA world (volatile, uncertain, complex and ambiguous). We've never gone through anything quite like this so you truly are navigating your way in unchartered waters. For some this ambiguity can be paralyzing. Finding a way to thrive in this new world takes a special blend of personality, perseverance and tenacity. But, to be honest, I don't believe the pandemic crisis *produced* these types of leaders. It simply revealed them—it showed who were the empty suits and who were the hidden gems. Much is right there beneath the surface but is only revealed through fire. What are these traits that made a way for some to thrive while others folded? During my own, long entrepreneurial journey of setting up high performance framework for fortune 500 companies and training more than 100,000 people to be exceptional leaders, I have identified four universal keys necessary to lead confidently in any season:

1. Clarity

Clear focus and vision are essential to growth and leadership in every season. This was true in my first business, AstroWix, a project management training and consulting company where we had 250 people on staff. It still holds true today 20 years later in my publishing business with a small team.

When you as a leader have a clear vision, when you have clarity of where you want to lead your business it becomes easier to show the same vision to your team. Clarity means having a destination in mind. It's knowing where you want to go. If you don't know where you are going a map will not help you. Clarity is knowing why you are in business; this is your purpose, your reason for existence.

Everything else flows from this clear vision. You need clarity to create your message to market and to deliver value to your customers. Good leaders know that their clarity (or lack of it) will trickle down to the rest of the team and eventually to the client. A good leader can cut through the complexity and endless distractions and other options in order to communicate a clear, direct and simple strategic vision for the entire organization. That clear vision informs its priorities and educates the rest of team on the mission. Such clarity guides the everyday actions, which clearly hits your bottom line. If you don't see the numbers that you want in your bottom line then going all the way back to revisiting the clarity of your vision might be a good idea! When you can express your vision in simple terms, remind yourself of it constantly, and get your team to buy into the same, clear vision, people tend to follow you, work with you, and buy from you with confidence.

Apple is a perfect example of this. If you pay attention, you will see that they always lead their marketing with their why and follow their own value of creating simple, elegant products that people are willing to pay premium for. The clarity of vision has built a loyal following.

On a personal level, I saw the clarity principle play out in my own work. As I look back on my project management business, I can see that we were thriving when we were focused and knew our why: the art of getting things done. We wanted to empower individuals and businesses to execute their projects on time, on target and within budget. This clear vision drove us.

A key to growing and learning for me has been the realization that clarity (along with these other leadership qualities) is not only necessary to effectively lead your team and your organization. It is imperative to have these key traits for yourself as the leader first. The vision trickles down. This has been validated by the leaders I have interviewed on my podcast, *Break Free to Brilliance*.

It is important to pause from time to time and look at your why. Are you still in alignment with it?

The best way I have found to gain clarity in alignment to myself is through meditation. Even two minutes a day can make a big difference. It is centering and brings an awareness to you, helping you be more present. Such practices allow you to be in tune with your intuition from which you can lead—especially in times of crisis.

You can apply creative ideas to complex situations in simple ways. Since I have been leading ***Master Your Inner Game*** meditations my clients and I have had tremendous growth in business and in the way of **being** that is true to our nature and led to our path. In fact, it has helped them see where they have gone off course and realign them to their original vision.

2. Connection

The second key quality is **connection**. Connection is how you relate and build relationships with others. In my own experience, the best results came when I was open and authentic to who I am. My uniqueness is my strength. This was a relief because I had years of experience of being me!! You can only pretend to be what others expect you to be for so long. People always find out when you are not your true self. Pretending or living by others' expectations also requires a lot of energy and effort, distracting you from your vision. Instead of wasting energy there, focus on being connected to your true self by upgrading your skills, knowledge and technology so you can be a better leader.

Hence, the first person to be fully connected with is yourself. I find this to be the first and foremost relationship you must build. It's about your own awareness of who you are at the core: how do you show up for the things that are important to you? What are your core values? What do you stand for?

Emotional Intelligence is a great tool to use to not only recognize, understand and be aware of your own emotions, but others' as well. The term emotional intelligence was created by two researchers, Peter Salavoy and John Mayer in their article "Emotional Intelligence" in the journal *Imagination, Cognition, and Personality* in 1990. It was later popularized by Dan Goleman in his 1996 book *Emotional Intelligence*.

Goleman shared that those emotions precede thoughts. Emotions change the way our brain functions, especially when in state of high emotions . . . it diminishes your cognitive abilities, decision-making powers and even interpersonal skills. Understanding and managing our emotions (and the emotions of others) helps us to be more successful in both our personal and professional lives.

Emotional intelligence both in personal and work situations helps us

- Have crucial conversations with ease and being objective
- Manage emotions in times of stress and overwhelm
- Improve relationships and become more collaborative
- Build psychological safety

Building Self-awareness is the key; emotions drive behavior, and understanding how others react to your behavior and vice versa can make a big impact on the results your leadership is driving. This can allow you to effortlessly connect with your team and clients. You have a natural calmness and roundedness about you that helps bring out the best in others.

Emotional Intelligence gives you the ability to have the crucial conversations without triggering emotions. It arms you with the courage to connect authentically. When teams can have an objective discussion honestly of what is working and not working, it has a huge impact on collaboration, creates healthy culture and affects the bottom line. Not to mention respect and admiration for you as a leader.

In 2003 Harvard Business Review reported that 80% of competencies that differentiate top performers from others are in the domain of Emotional Intelligence.

Being connected to yourself at a deeper level, will allow you to effortlessly connect with your team and clients.

When you stand in your truth, it naturally gives others the permission, comfort, ease and grace to do the same. The result is collectively delivering high performance.

In my experience, such connection is one of our greatest assets. I saw incredible success by being able to link with people at any level, whether they came from a small rural town or from one of the major cities throughout the world. The common denominator I have found is that people want to be understood, seen and heard. When you keep this in mind, you won't have any issues connecting with people.

Last month I got a call from one our technical team members who worked with us 20 years ago in New Delhi, India, on Microsoft's Project Management software—EPM. He is now working with a major corporation in the US. He was reflecting on how we were able to connect with each employee, see the dreams and vision they had for their own life, tie it with the company's vision, and lead them to success. He came from a small town, didn't speak English, and had very little work experience. He appreciated the fact that despite the team size of 250 people we made time to know who he was and personally mentored him. Twenty years later we are still in touch with many of the people that worked with us then. All because we knew the value of connection—then and now.

3. Conversion

Clarity and connection are critical in the foundation of our leadership. The next ingredient to make our leadership successful is the magic of converting. It is both about doing the work of converting and seeing the sparkle in someone's eye at the moment conversion happens. Conversion is making progress. It is the ability to get buy-in to your idea or concept. Typically, this term is used in sales because it is related to that moment when your vision translates into the bottom line. When you translate your vision so well that you connect with the consumer and actually change their action.

It means that you have shown each team member why their role was an important factor in the overall vision. As they bought in, they connected it with others and it rippled out to impact the world.

Here is a story that might resonate with you:

Two brick layers were working side by side constructing a temple.

An older gentleman walked by and asked the first brick layer, "What are you doing?"

The first brick layer replied, "I am laying bricks; isn't it obvious by what you are seeing?"

The older gentleman asked the second brick layer, "What are you doing?"

The second brick layer replied with a big smile, "I am building a temple!"

Two brick layers. Two very different answers. The second brick layer had been converted to the vision. Who do you think will do the best work and go the extra mile to make the vision of a new temple a reality? When your team understands how they fit in the bigger vision, they will have ownership and pride in what they do, creating a final product with greater value.

Converting is a continuous process that needs to be done at least a few times a year and particularly in times of change and crisis. Do you have a list of items that need to be converted to gain real value?

4. Adaptability and Vulnerability

Adaptability simply means being agile. It is the art of thinking on your feet and even changing direction mid-journey. This is easier to do when you have a clear destination in mind. When you have clarity of vision and a basic roadmap in place, rerouting is much easier to navigate. Your initial roadmap probably has some plans for known unknowns and semi-unknowns—these are the risks that you have not encountered yet but can anticipate as possible risks for your industry. You cannot plan for the unknown unknowns like a pandemic. But when you have the others identified and a plan in place, you and your team are better equipped to handle the unknown unknowns. This season has been a great lesson on this.

Vulnerability means allowing people to see the authentic, human side of you. Humility and vulnerability might appear as weakness to some. In truth, they are the core strengths of a leader. As Brenee Brown has shown us, "Vulnerability is the *courage* to take a risk and put yourself out there, especially when you can't control the outcome. Humility accompanies it and is the *strength* to admit that even if you're the leader, you don't have all the answers. Good leaders know that together the team will find the best possible solution for the organization." I have learned that courage comes when you step into your power.

My husband is good at this. During our years in project management together, he was never afraid to show that he didn't know what to do when we were in a critical situation. He always said, "I don't know what to do right now, but if we look at our past, we have had success and have faith in God, in myself and in you. I know that together we will come up with a solution. If we don't get the desired results, we still have won because this will be a great lesson for all of us!" He said it with such certainty that we all felt grounded and re-energized for the task at hand. We pulled the curtain back and taught them as we learned. As our employees moved on in their career many of them became successful entrepreneurs.

Adaptability and vulnerability work in tandem because they both assume challenges and imperfections will come. A good leader doesn't have to be perfect. A good leader just has to have the courage to be real and make changes when they are needed so that the destination stays in view even if the original roadmap needs to be rerouted.

In summary there are four keys to being an exceptional leader in any season.

They are: **clarity, connection, conversion, and adaptability and vulnerability**.

If you employ these four keys—whether you are in a season of crisis or of stability—your value as a leader will shine as a true gem and the people you lead will be blessed. Some of these traits may come naturally to you. Others may need your devoted attention. Take a moment to create a plan for your own growth in each of these keys.

Seema Giri

Seema Giri is an international best-selling and award-winning author, international speaker, book writing mentor and publisher. Over the last 20 years, she has helped more than 100,000 spiritually aligned entrepreneurs and leaders expand their consciousness, tap into their inner power, and unleash their true potential so that they become unstoppable in business and life. Drawing from her own experiences with chronic illness, isolation and deep feelings of emptiness and defeat, Seema offers insight and hope to leaders who want to shine.

After years of honing her craft and sharing her own story, her latest endeavor is to help others come out of the shadows by telling their own stories. She helps leaders and entrepreneurs expand their influence and impact through her *Shine Your Brilliance as an Author* program and storytelling platform. Her clients write high-impact books—sharing wisdom they gained from life-altering experiences. As they do, the lives of readers are transformed, making a massive positive impact in the world.

Her expertise comes from a vast storehouse of experiences and opportunities including traveling around the world. In addition to her own book projects and speaking engagements, she is proud to have co-authored the book *The Authorities*, with *New York Times* best selling authors Dr. John Gray (*Men are from Mars Women are from Venus*), Marci Shimoff (*Happiness for No Reason*), and Raymond Aaron (*Double Your Income Doing What You Love*). In it she chronicles her transformation from being bed ridden and in chronic pain to becoming a successful entrepreneur, mother and wife. The rare combination of her personal testimony and her extensive expertise makes her a skilled and hopeful guide to all who want to tell their own stories and impact the world.

FB Page: Break Free to Authority, Impact & Influence with Seema Giri
LinkedIn: **www.linkedin.com/in/BreakFreetoBrilliance**
Instagram: **https://www.instagram.com/giriseema1**
Shine Your Brilliance FB group: **https://www.facebook.com/groups/shineyourbrilliance**
YouTube: **http://bit.ly/BreakFree2BrillianceChannel**
Podcast: Break Free to Brilliance at your favorite podcast listening platform
Check out Author Opportunities: **https://www.seemagiri.com/bookwritingopportunities/**
Website: **https://www.uplyft.media**

PART 2:
TRANSFORMATIONAL LEADER

POWER OF THREE FOR TRANSFORMATIONAL LEADERSHIP

UPENDRA GIRI

"We need to learn to love ourselves first, in all our glory and our imperfections. If we cannot love ourselves, we cannot fully open to our ability to love others or our potential to create. Evolution and all hopes for a better world rest in the fearlessness and open-hearted vision of people who embrace life."
—John Lennon

Life is not perfect, and we are not perfect either. The idea of imperfection is the steppingstone to a highly creative process in the universe. My life journey was far from perfect. Starting my journey in a small village in India with not many privileges led to fearlessness and unique vision which created something I never imagined. I learned lessons in the zone of imperfection, and even now these lessons hold true and are guiding light to me in every circumstance. I believe the sooner we stop chasing perfection, the earlier we start living with imperfections and create something magical.

Every facet of life, including how we work, is not an anomaly to this fact. Chasing perfectionism is an iron-fisted grip that can cause unrealistic goals and creates a veil through which we can't see our creative self.

Today, many organizations are going through a transformational process that requires specific, frequently perfect changes to position them for sustained success. Today, these changes are more complex and happening at a faster pace than ever before. Organizations are trying to adapt to change while also accommodating the more incredible speed and complexity of the change.

A Chase to Be Perfect

It's counter-intuitive, but organizations need to weigh the options between being perfect or creative and become the ground that gives creativity a boost. In my entrepreneurial journey I chose to be the latter and hired more than 500 employees from the lower to middle-class income bracket in India in my first successful startup AstroWix Corporation in the late '90s. Now I recall that a small decision of choosing the imperfect became the very reason for continuous transformation and created a foreground of my success. Choosing the path of humility and courage became the DNA at the boutique firm, making a streak of productivity and performance management possible.

My Submission – The Culture Matters

Organizations leave tremendous potential on the table if they are not focusing on the culture. Based on my experience with the first company I set up with my wife in the late '90s, what is true even now is that strategy, structure, process and technology are critical aspects for organization growth. To harness the potential of the people in the organization, one must hire, develop and help them evolve.

Company culture, like personal character, is an amorphous quality that exerts a powerful influence. The company culture influences employees' leadership styles more than any other aspect of their jobs. A person learns, envisions, engages, and executes a project efficiently compared with people who do the same job but who work in different companies and carry foundations of cultural values.

What personally worked with me at a young age was;

- ***Inner Strength – Intuition, Thoughts & Feelings***

- ***Experiential Learning – Learn, Unlearn & Relearn***

- **OKRs – *Inputs, Outputs & Outcomes***

"You have power over your mind—not outside events.
Realize this, and you will find strength."
—Marcus Aurelius.

Inner strength has always been my backbone and savior in challenging circumstances. I tell my kids that when you talk to yourself, say I am proud of myself and did my best. If you fail to get yes to this statement even once, you need to reflect and check your actions. To awaken this strong spirit of resilience, your conscious self should be evident. If you are mindful of your actions, you can build your inner strength based on that truth. It's imperative that you don't wait for the right time to strike so that you can start working on this strength. Build it so that once testing time strikes, you can summon all the strength inside you with just one thought. It's almost a Zen-like state where you look yourself deep inside to find the innate power.

My Intuition- When It's OK to Trust Your Gut on A Big Decision

As per Murphy's law, "Anything that can go wrong will go wrong." That is destiny or luck. I would instead call it a sequence of events that lead to one probability as an outcome.

So, what is the right way to tackle this uncertainty?

One will always have data, experience, and preparation at any given time. At the same time, one also has Intuition opening the door to more clarity, decisiveness, and connection—all essential to move forward. By honing one's intuition, you can elevate all your leadership skills. This approach is especially very useful in the absence of data or past experiences.

When I started my first startup, I had no experience running a company or even domain expertise; the idea just felt right to me. I had no access to any analytics, market research and big data that is available to an entrepreneur nowadays. Data govern everything to the point that it seems as though the human decision is not even present in the equation. As an entrepreneur who has made many decisions based on gut instinct, I'm afraid I disagree that all decisions should be taken based on data alone. For example, at one point in time, I was faced with a significant decision that could have either ruined the success of my business and career or skyrocketed it. I stared at the numbers, the facts, the projections, but the choice ultimately came down to following my intuition.

In my role as a business leader, I often see that whenever I ask for feedback about my opinions at work, most of my peers tend to agree with my point of view. Very few challenge it or ask 'why?' From early on in our lives, it is deeply ingrained in our minds to concede to authority, even if our instinct says otherwise. It is especially true in India, where the 'power gap' is among the highest in the world. However, doing so not only undermines one's perspective but leads to ignoring one's gut instinct that more often than not points you in the right direction.

We must learn to trust our instincts and have faith in these small signals from the universe. The question is: how do we begin this journey to understand our instincts and transform our thought process?

There are two types of decisions that are not dependent on Intuition. One is where the data is known, and options can be calculated or estimated to the closest possibility.

The other are decisions with a long track record of experience behind them; however, even this type of decision may require more than just experience, as the future is different from the past. The only thing to keep in mind is that blunders happen due to biases. A gut feeling can be pretty accurate if these biases are minimized by considering these plausible facts.

Hence, intuition plays an essential role in rapidly changing environments; there are contradictions in the data, ambiguity due to lack of data or decisions that center around people (hiring, firing or political decisions). Ironically, the fact is that data alone isn't enough for some decisions, which should never be overlooked. Most leaders today use all the data at their disposal, input from a wide range of sources, and yet they listen to the voice inside their heads. The fusion of cognition and intuition is powerful for all business leaders to create a successful organization.

My Thoughts – Pursue Self-Mastery

Over the years, I realized that Self-mastery raises your level of consciousness and controls the thought process that ultimately guides your emotions, habits, and behaviors. Developing self-mastery can radically improve your performance both at work and in your personal life. Self-limiting, fear-based thoughts that produce negative emotions also limit performance. Thoughts create your reality but also have the power to reduce focus and confidence. When I reflect on the past, I outperformed when I was centered around an inner state of the "flow" or "fluidity," key to performing optimally. When you increase your self-mastery, you improve all aspects of your life, both personally and professionally.

Self-mastery is captured well by Meryl Streep in the quote:

"Watch your thoughts; they become words;
Watch your words; they become actions;
Watch your actions; they become habits;
Watch your habits; they become character;
Watch your character, for it becomes your destiny."

Self-Mastery is not easy; it requires hard work, patience, truthfulness, purity, impeccability and faith in oneself. It is one road which when taken is worthy enough to pay the price.

My Feelings - Listen to Your Body

The human body is the most complex system, and like every system, it follows a specific process to sustain and grow. If dealt with care, it can be an extraordinary tool to harbor a spirit of hope. What helped me the most during my life is remembering that anxiousness and anxiety happening to the body is the essential element for our protection. These affect the mind and the heart, the physical body and the "energy body." Energy body for people who are new to the concept can be understood simply as how energy flows for optimum human existence in a body. It is the best coping mechanism that focuses on the body and bypasses the mind.

Humans tend to be in fight or flight mode to combat difficult situations. Centering oneself in the present if you want to empower yourself to do different activities and adjust to other conditions is extremely important.

Meditation has been known for its benefits since time immemorial. It starts with listening to your emotions and not thinking that it's wrong to be anxious. Instead, your body is trying to say something every second of existence and its only goal is to grow.

Source: Positive Psychology

Experiential Learning – Learn, Unlearn & Relearn

The key is creating a winning culture of continuous learning in the company. I am a lifelong learner on this journey! Learning agility is the name of the game for any organization. Unlearn starts with focusing on letting go of old rules. The rules are changing fast; your ability to be agile in letting go of old traditions and learning new ones becomes increasingly essential. Agility is the key to unlocking your change proficiency and succeeding in an uncertain, unpredictable and constantly evolving environment, both personally and professionally. To relearn the new rules and bring a passion for inspiring critical thinking in your organization. Keep this dialogue going for deep thought and winning culture.

Learn, Unlearn and Relearn is my evolution mantra!

The continuous learning culture increases knowledge, competence and performance continually, and innovation of individuals and organizations. Through learning, we can do something we never were able to do. Through education, we re-perceive the world and create a new relationship with it. We become an essential part of the regenerative process of life by being open to the process of learning.

Why is lifelong learning culture a stepping stone to organization success?

Individuals, teams and enterprises today face challenges that create both uncertainty and opportunity. The exponential pace of technology innovation is convincing. Teams in the organizations can challenge the status quo by transforming, disrupting and in some cases eliminating entire markets. The political, economic and environmental landscape threatens to change the rules of the game. Startups are expected to think and act beyond balance sheets and quarterly earnings reports. Due to these factors, we all need to adapt rapidly and continuously or face decline—and ultimately extinction.

What's the solution?

Adapt to the current climate with continuous learning at all levels. Organizations should leverage the collective knowledge, experience and creativity of their workforce and other stakeholders in the ecosystem. Curiosity, exploration, invention, entrepreneurship and informed risk-taking replace commitment to the status quo while providing stability and predictability. Fluid organizational constructs that can shift as needed to optimize the flow of value rather than a rigid structure can decentralize decision-making. This flow focuses on vision and strategy while enabling organization members to achieve their fullest potential.

Leaders may think that a clear vision and providing employees lots of training is enough. This assumption is flawed and risky in the face of intensifying competition. Unless the growth mindset at the level of organization is achieved along with open communication, it can become difficult for an organization to reach a whole new realm of benefits that can catalyze the transition from traditional corporation to the new-age one.

OKRs – Inputs, Outputs & Outcomes

OKRs, or "objectives and key results," are a popular goal managing framework that can help teams set measurable yet ambitious goals. OKRs create results that matter most for the organizations to increase cultural transparency. OKRs can enable teams to focus on primary objectives and accomplish more than they thought was possible, even if they don't fully attain the stated goal. To increase employee engagement and help your teams set and achieve ambitious goals, try setting OKRs. It helps leave comfort zones, prioritize work and learn from both success and failure. Netflix, Adobe and Google have all implemented OKRs to create successful milestones. Tangible, objective and unambiguous key results are a powerful way to set the goals of any company.

Most individuals, teams and organizations find the Key Results in one of three categories: Inputs, Outputs and Outcomes. Most times Inputs are things that you can control. Some leaders only focus on Inputs. They believe that if the right Inputs are considered, desired Outcomes will follow. Outputs are the effects of your inputs. Outputs are what people produce; outcomes are the impacts that are created because of the value a company has delivered. While outcomes are more meaningful, a business must get there with outputs.

Outcomes are usually more complex than an Output. A good Outcome addresses the underlying challenge you are solving more directly than an Input or Output.

As a startup, I was able to leverage the power of OKRs, leading to increased employee performance. It led to easy implementation of projects and created a strategy that revolved entirely around the key results. In the beginning it was all about deliverables and output but as we mastered the art and science of OKRs, it all became outcomes and value realization for individuals, teams and organization.

OKRs empower teams to set goals that stretch beyond BAU - or "business as usual" - and make significant, meaningful change. When implemented effectively, OKRs can provide many benefits, including clarity, enhanced communication, and a coherent, transparent organization-wide strategy.

Upendra Giri

Upendra Giri is known for his entrepreneurial mindset and capability with a rare blend of innovation and unwavering determination to bring products to market, known for influencing change, building great talent, monetizing opportunities, and executing relentlessly with customer- centricity. He is an award winning international best seller, coach, trainer and serial entrepreneur who helps senior leaders from Bay Area to Bengaluru transform their organizations to achieve more innovation, collaboration and business agility. At present Upendra is CEO and Founder of UpLyft Global, committed to helping individuals, teams and organizations on their transformation journey. Upendra has been instrumental in laying down the foundation of project management in India. In 2009, he was awarded the prestigious Eric Jennet Award by PMI® for his outstanding contributions to the global portfolio, program and project management profession. He is the first Indian and the youngest professional who has been bestowed this award to date. A true leader, evangelist and professional engineer, he is also the Founder and Trustee of PMI® North India Chapter and is Charter Member of TiE. Upendra earned his MS in Civil (Environmental) Engineering from Lehigh University, PA, USA in 1994 and B.Sc. in Civil Engineering in 1991 from Jamia Millia Islamia University, New Delhi, India. Born in 1969 in a village in northern India, Upendra now resides in Silicon Valley, US and is one of the most sought-after consultants by CEOs of big multinational companies.

Upendra travels globally to speak at business and technology events and shares his vision for transforming individuals, teams and organizations for unleashing their potentials.

https://www.linkedin.com/in/upendragiri/
https://www.facebook.com/upendra.giri.752
https://www.UpLyftGlobal.com/

LEADERSHIP THE FEMININE WAY
CONNECTION – COLLABORATION – COMMUNITY

ANDREA WOOLF

From my very first full-time job, I worked directly with either managers, senior executives or business owners.

This was where I was destined to be. With hindsight, it gave me the enormous opportunity to learn all about leadership experientially which is my favorite learning style—both from non-communicative, unappreciative and mediocre leaders, as well as amazing, inspiring and phenomenal leaders.

I realized early on that I would never want to be that mediocre leader, disconnected from my team, not including them in visioning or planning and expecting them to be psychic to boot!

There is only one way I wanted to be, learned from my wonderfully perfectionist mother—and that is to give 100% effort to everything I do, nothing less. In addition, I am extremely loyal, at times way over the top. In more than one position, I overstayed for years, even though I had stood still both role-wise and reward.

I believe strongly that there are no accidents. That my early career laid the groundwork for me to discover my purpose—what I am here on the planet to do—and to step into my dream life, launching my own business as a zesty business and personal coach over twenty-five years ago.

What a difference! I have been at the helm of my own ship, ongoingly stretching and growing. And I have truly loved every minute of every day ever since!

Here are some key lessons in leadership that I have learned along the way, both as a team member as well as a business and personal coach:

6 Keys to Impactful Leadership

- **Be the Visionary** - Have a clear vision/big picture and include everyone in it

- **Value People in Words and in Deeds** - In every area of your life

- **Show that You Care** - Acknowledge people often

- **Stay True to Your Values** - Be aligned with them in business and in life

- **Be Trusting and Trustworthy**

- **Lead by Example** - Walk your talk

Since I am an experiential learner, these 6 Keys are not just made up—they come from being tested and proven in my business and life.

For example, one of the first big ones was, "Stay True to Your Values." I was working for a husband and wife team in their small manufacturing company, primarily for the wife. She was not the easiest person to work for, regularly moody and prickly. Somehow, though, I managed to successfully work with her for almost three years.

One fine day she called me into her office, looking more uncomfortable than usual. Not looking me in the eye, she handed me a document and, talking faster than usual, she asked me to white out one line and replace it with different data and a larger dollar number, then copy it.

It was only when I got back to my desk that I realized that this was an insurance claim form that she was asking me to alter. I felt a pit in my stomach and it took me no more than ten seconds to realize that there was no way I could do anything that was so "not okay."

I have come to know that my top three values are: Integrity, Love and Full Self-Expression.

At the same time, I was extremely concerned as I needed the job. I was supporting family members at the time. I took a deep breath, and immediately went back to her office to let her know as tactfully as I could that there was no way that I could do it as I'm not honest just "sometimes" when it's "convenient," I'm honest *all of the time*—and I handed the document back to her. She turned red and purple and I thought that the end was nigh. If looks could kill I would not be here right now.

I immediately went to her husband's office to let him know, and he listened nodding, then told me not to worry. It would all be okay. While that turned out to be true and I did not get fired, it served as the catalyst for me to start looking that same day for my next adventure—for which I will be forever grateful.

I learned from this experience to stay true to myself no matter what, to walk my talk and to live my values. And I have done that very consciously ever since.

I have learned in my life that it's only at times like this one that I have truly realized who I am, what I stand for and whether I am living my values or not. And if not, I quickly course correct.

My next adventure was a significant improvement regarding integrity, however there were other challenges to test me. I was the right-hand person to a renowned, highly successful architect. I supported him to keep the business running smoothly and maintain excellent relationships with the team, important clients and their teams, as well as prospects and the media.

Over the three years that I was with him my job actually quadrupled, until I was also taking care of the entire architectural team as well as him. Despite this, my reward remained the same. At every annual review, he found a creative way to avoid the topic or change the subject. And while he sang my praises and expressed appreciation for my dedication, he failed to do anything to show me he meant it in any meaningful way.

It was my last review that was the catalyst for me to wake up. As I entered his office I could tell he was extremely uncomfortable. He was bright red, sweating slightly and would not look me in the eye. As I sat down, he looked away and then informed me that he had received complaints about me.

I was in shock and asked him who it was so I could immediately resolve whatever the issue was with them. Still not looking at me, he said he could not tell me. I knew something was up. Miraculously I connected with my inner wise woman, and asked him if he wouldn't tell me *who* it was, would he share with me *what* it was, again so that I could resolve the matter. As he got redder and redder and more and more uncomfortable it suddenly hit me that this was all to avoid giving me a raise and/or a bonus. I stood up and left him squirming in his office.

It turned out that no one had complained about me. I had guessed right. He simply did not want to increase my reward, and he chose a cowardly way out.

I finally got the message! He did not value me. It was time to move on.

On that very same day I contacted the agency that had placed me there. They were delighted to hear from me and quickly matched me with what was to be the biggest opportunity of my life to date.

This last job before I started my own business proved to be the most important teacher of all.

I worked for the Vice Chairman of a multinational corporation, a leader in its field. He was the third in command of this huge global enterprise. I was with him for five years in the same period that he was taking the company public. This meant that he was traveling all over the world all the time doing mergers and acquisitions, as well as significantly growing the divisions that serviced the company worldwide. He was truly a visionary, both brilliant and imposing.

I went through five interviews to get the job, the fifth one being with him. The interview was rather like having dental surgery without an anesthetic. Over several hours he kept asking me in all kinds of creative ways how I would handle it if something went wrong under my watch.

How refreshing! It was clear to me that he was checking out my integrity, and whether I could be trusted. He had clearly had some bad experiences prior to me.

In turn I found various ways to assure him I would assess the situation, come up with ways to resolve it, then find him wherever he was in the world, and get his agreement on next steps.

We turned out to be a match made in heaven. He was even more of a perfectionist than I was!

My job supporting this wonderful man instantly became massive. It was on a global level. And not only could nothing go wrong under my watch, everything was urgent!

With hindsight, what it took to pull it off was 100% possibility thinking. Nothing less.

And unbeknownst to me at the time, what great training for becoming a coach and starting my business.

It was while I was there that I discovered the field of coaching at a time long ago when no one had heard of it.

I often worked until 10 or 11 pm at night, and often on the weekends, so I kept a fully stocked kitchen in the worldwide corporate headquarters at all times. Word spread fast and I made a number of good friends who were as crazy as me and would stop by to have a snack and chat in the evening.

A wonderful man on the marketing team came by one evening and shared that he was going to be leaving. I took him out for lunch on his last day and, lo and behold, I discovered that he was leaving to go build his coaching practice which was unheard of at that time.

As he was telling me about coaching, I had a full body chill. I knew I was meeting my destiny, discovering what I'm here on the planet to do. I realized I have been coaching my whole life!

When I was very young, around 3 or 4, my mother was a hairdresser and I loved to go with her to her salon and chat with her clients. They would share with me their biggest challenge and I would help them to create a step to take that week. Then I would check in with them the following week to find out how they got on. In other words, I was coaching them even at that young age!

I hired my buddy on the spot, without asking what he charged, nor having a clue what I was letting myself in for.

I had this gnawing feeling that there had to be more to life than just my job, which was ironic as I had little to no life outside of work. Since he knew me so well, his first assignment was for me to leave early one night. I was so out of whack it took me three weeks to do it!

Working with my buddy and first coach, with his help and by design, I picked a date 18 months out to leave the company and launch my coaching practice. In the interim I would get trained as a coach.

Miracle of miracles, it played out exactly that way and on that exact day! Everything was completely planned and amicable. I have not looked back since. It has been over 25 years now, and it has been an amazing journey. I have loved every minute of serving and supporting amazing women just like you to "Love the life you live, Live the life you love."

Leadership the Feminine Way is to do it ***your*** way—the way that comes naturally to you.

Here is how to step into being the highly effective, powerful leader you are destined to be:

5 Simple Tips to Lead the Feminine Way

1. **Embrace Your Magnificence!** – Step into your power so you radiate confidence, authority and joy. In turn you will inspire everyone around you to do the same. So be contagious!

2. **Collaborate** – Create a collaborative culture around yourself. It will be much more effective and infinitely more fun. Being inclusive is the best way to lead. Everyone gets to participate and contribute, and they will never leave!

3. **Lead with Love** – Open your heart and lead from there to access caring, kindness and compassion. This is your true strength and magic secret sauce!

4. **Communicate to Connect** – Listen openly so others feel heard, and lean in to show you are interested. In addition, be uplifting, understanding and inspiring when you speak.

5. **Trust Yourself** – Listen to your wise inner voice, also known as your instincts. When you trust yourself, you naturally create a ripple of trust all around you. Be that ripple and watch what happens . . .

The world is waiting for you to step into your power, and stand up, speak out and shine. Be the feminine leader extraordinaire you are here to be, and make the huge impact you are here to make.

To your magnificence!

Andrea Woolf

Andrea Woolf

From the moment Andrea Woolf discovered the field of coaching it was like finding the glove that fit her. She knew immediately that this was the contribution she was here to make. One of the first assignments Andrea completed with her very first coach was to design her transition out of the corporate world. Eighteen months later, almost to the date she had created in her vision, Andrea launched her business and personal coaching practice which has successfully flourished over the last several decades.

With her heartfelt style she has helped hundreds of women to clarify, simplify and achieve extraordinary results while bringing purpose and meaning to every aspect of their lives. Each day Andrea fulfills her dream of inspiring amazing women to transform their lives, and truly connect to the difference they make in the world.

Andrea is also a motivational speaker and trainer, and the author of ***Ignite Your Life! – How to Get from Where You Are to Where You Want to Be.***

She is the founder of **Ignited Women of Impact**, a vibrant community of women entrepreneurs and executives ready to change the world and, in the process, take their business or career and entire life to a whole new level. She inspires women to go from settling to *sizzling*, so they stand up, speak out and shine in the world!

And to fulfill her dream of helping women get their voices out into the world, she is the host of her podcast, ***Ignited Women of Impact – Amazing Women with Inspiring Stories.***

website: **www.andreawoolf.com**
email: **andrea@andreawoolf.com**

A LIFE TRANSFORMED: FROM A FOLLOWER TO A LEADER

MARSHA CHEUNG GOLANGCO

As an immigrant to the United States from Hong Kong, I grew up never having thought of myself as a leader or learned what it meant to be "a leader."

I was the youngest daughter of seven. Born in the lunar year of the Ox, on

the last day of the leap month of July, it was a date that was neither auspicious nor inauspicious. It was just another ordinary day, and another ordinary life. I was neither expected to be extraordinary nor excel in life on my own. I was not expected to become someone of importance—only perhaps to marry one who is.

Despite the good education I received growing up in Hong Kong and a few college degrees in the United States, I never focused my energy pursuing any high positions in corporations. After all, I was only a woman with seemingly little importance. Furthermore, in my culture, the male is considered to be more important, usually holding positions of power and always having the advantage of advancement over the female. To stay true to my family's and culture's expectation, I became a traditional homemaker and focused on taking care of my three children. Occasionally, I worked full time to break up the monotony, but it never felt fulfilling enough. In my perception of myself, I was not good enough to do anything of significance.

My turning point came when a close friend invited me to attend a self-discovery program. I gradually realized that I had been wasting my precious time and energy, focusing on the negative aspects of life. I was surprised to find out that I was actually a person with multiple talents and something to offer. I unearthed a sense of creativity and discovered the many positive attributes to lead a fulfilling, powerful life.

With my initial breakthroughs, I continued to further develop myself, turning negatives into positives. I learned that being positive will lead to confident and constructive actions. In addition to furthering my own personal growth and development, I started to become active in community affairs, volunteering my time and efforts in helping different non-profit organizations. I became a community advocate focusing on many issues, such as anti-violence and hate, while promoting peace and harmony. Gaining confidence and self-esteem, I became known as an effective leader, eventually being invited to serve in different leadership roles in numerous non-profit associations, including becoming a co-founder of two sustainable green organizations.

In acknowledgement of my community contributions, I received several significant awards, including an honorable mention for the Martin Luther King Jr. Humanitarian Award of the Year in 2005 and the Asian American Award of the Year in 2020.

Another unexpected accomplishment was becoming a Feng Shui Expert in the building industry. Due to my early family introduction to the ancient discipline of Feng Shui, I was able to integrate that knowledge into the modern construction designing process, helping builders to greatly enhance their products. Eventually I wrote three books called *The Power of Feng Shui Trilogy*, and recently became an international best-selling author with two anthologies.

All these successes would not have happened if I did not overcome challenges by turning my negative thinking into positive actions and making wise choices in life. I would not have become a leader in my community if I chose to live small and think lowly of myself.

A Leader of All Seasons

After many years as a community leader, I now consider myself an All-Weather Leader instead of a Good-Weather Leader. When I first began developing my own leadership skills, I found myself intentionally avoiding confrontational situations. I would keep quiet, not wanting to voice my opinion for fear of offending anyone. I later learned that these actions are not beneficial in resolving a problem because the problem would still exist. As a true leader, it is better to have the courage to tell the truth, or to disagree. Strong leaders are not people pleasers trying to avoid responsibilities. Strong leaders will continue to develop skills to face challenges and difficulties instead of running away.

Leadership training is a long and continuous process, with the intent of providing service and contribution to others. When we are willing to shift our focus from self to others, and when we are willing to face challenging life issues powerfully and with courage, we take responsibility to become the source that makes a difference. We will authentically be expressing ourselves as a true leader of all seasons!

Continuity of Leadership

True Leadership does not stop with oneself. It continues to flourish on different levels, from self to family, to community, to the nation and to the world!

A good leader starts from oneself and manifests into the desire to serve and contribute to others. Do no harm and do good are basic principles; always consciously make decisions that are positive and constructive to self and others. Actions are generated from love, kindness and compassion. Forming a solid foundation with daily healthy self-care is vital. A good leader is physically strong, mentally clear, emotionally stable, financially abundant and has a reputation of integrity.

It is important to connect and collaborate with others even if there are disagreements. Continue to find a common ground to form alliances with others. There are many leaders throughout history who resolved differences with intolerance; this led to hate and violence and ultimately to a dead end.

It would be a wiser decision to resolve differences with patience, empathy and a peaceful approach to reduce chaos during social unrest. A true leader follows these valuable guiding principles to unite, form alliances and work together to overcome difficulties, regardless of differences.

Mentoring young generations to lead is an important approach to continue a network of successful leaders. Young people are like small plants: when nurtured in favorable environments, they grow and develop into strong trees. When young people are trained as true leaders, they become responsible with the intention to serve and contribute in a beneficial way!

Nowadays, numerous community organizations offer Youth Leadership programs, which teach basic leadership skills such as communication in speaking and writing, cognitive thinking and team building to encourage working together. Other programs place youth into political offices and community organizations to intern, learning real life experiences. More recently, these programs are exploring the ethics of leadership, asking profound questions like: why do young people want to be leaders? What would they provide for others? What could be considered as true leadership?

I am excited to see that the Youth Leadership Program I developed six years ago with APAPA (Asian Pacific Islander American Public Affairs Association) Tri Valley chapter is improving every year. Through this program, multiple generations will receive valuable training, then move on with their lives with the power to serve and contribute!

Reflection of My Own Leadership Pathway

It is not an easy pathway to evolve from a follower to a leader.

In summary, let me quote from a paper I published in the *Journal of the Conference for Global Transformation* entitled, "Living an Impossible Promise in an Imperfect World, Challenges & Fulfillment."

"When I first noticed that I was restless and unhappy with myself, my family, my job and everything occurred as a boredom to me, I realized these were the signs of stagnancy in life. I could see them as signals to move on and to make new changes. I left my secure job in a big corporation, created a consulting work in cultural education, and later became known as a Feng Shui expert. I started taking skill-building, self-discovery and self-improvement courses.

All this life empowerment training allowed me to recognize the constraints from my past that were still limiting my life. As an immigrant from Asia now an American naturalized citizen, I realized I inherited cultural values demanding women to be passive and dependent. I could see that being complacent and playing safe was not my true commitment in life.

What I really wanted was to achieve my authentic self-expression, and to live fully and powerfully in a way that would make differences in the world around me!

Giving up the past constraining beliefs gave me a new responsibility in life. That responsibility for generating a supportive environment for myself transformed me from a passive, self-absorbed individual to a community-minded person. I was able to break away from my traditional mode into an independent, self-reliant person with a passion to serve. After years of active participation in community advocacy, I am now recognized as a true contributor of my community."

When we take the lead in our own lives, we become open to a greater life for ourselves and others in the world!

Marsha Cheung Golangco

Marsha Cheung Golangco is a bestselling author, speaker and consultant in Environmental Feng Shui and Sustainable Green Building Advisory. She is also a social entrepreneur and a longtime community advocate. Her mission is to promote a harmonious world that works for all. For many years, Marsha has used her knowledge and wisdom in helping others to create favorable and healthy living environments for a better quality of life.

Committed to a lifetime contribution to the ongoing global peace and the sustainable green movement, Marsha continues to develop a local-to-global collaboration through her business and community advocacy. She serves in many local-to-global organizations, including USGBC (United States Green Building Council, East Bay, California), Chairperson of the

Board of Director of APAPA (Asian American Islander American Public Affairs Association) Tri Valley Chapter and Cofounders of Sustainable Contra Costa and Sustainable Walnut Creek, California.

For her many community contributions, Marsha received numerous awards, including the President's Award of the Year of the Building Industry Association for her dedication to the advancement of professional women in the building industry. She is a recipient of an Honorable Mention Martin Luther King Jr. Humanitarian Award of the Year and the Asian American Islander American of the Year (APIA) in 2020.

Sharing her knowledge and wisdom in the Eastern culture, Marsha co-authored two bestselling anthologies and is the author of *The Power of Feng Shui Trilogy*:

The Power of Feng Shui for Builders

The Power of Feng Shui for Your Life

The Power of Feng Shui for Green Living

Marsha can be reached at **fengshu888@aol.com**.
Website: **www.windwater888.com**
Facebook: **facebook.com/marsha.golangco**
LinkedIn: **www.linkedin.com/in/marsha-golangco**

TRANSFORMING IS KEY TO LEADING

MAURINE XAVIER

Fear comes up when I start to write.

What if I don't know what to do? What if I don't know what to say?

I have been terrified to be a writer because deep down I know something. I know writing is fun, and fun is something I haven't been willing to have. Being dismal has been more my style. Being in pain, miserable. That has been my life, and writing this chapter is bringing to the forefront that having fun is out of my comfort zone.

This is an example of leadership, being willing to tell the truth, when you catch yourself in living a lie.

Writing is a journey I didn't want to take because I think it means something to be a writer, a storyteller, a playwright. "I "am" a "meaning making machine." Storytelling is an art, a creation, and a possibility, and when you are attached to writing something meaningful, it's hard to tell a leadership story. I believe leadership requires courage, authenticity and willingness to tell the truth when you see it.

I haven't been willing to tell the truth, that I love writing. Writing is an example of a possibility. It doesn't have to mean anything unless you "are" a meaning making machine, like me. When you are a leader, you get to tell the difference between fact and fiction. That's what transformational leadership is, discovering the truth when other people don't see it.

I am a transformational leader. I tell the truth, even when it's not popular. I channel a team of Divine Guides and I have been a transformational student for a decade. This story I am writing is transformational leadership. The story I am writing is transformation. I discovered many things about me as I was dictating from the Guides, and I was willing to share it all here with you, every last detail.

My Divine Guide Team and I facilitate miracles every day. As I am writing that line, I hit a block. I realize I am self-conscious about talking about how talented I am. (I teared up and started to have that ugly girl cry.) I have been gifted and talented for all of my life, and I shut myself in the closet. I was afraid to show my talents because it was not acceptable.

As I write this line, I have a memory come up, so I stop and get present. I see a picture of myself getting slapped across the face for being too vocal, then the thought comes to me: "I will never do that again." (No wonder it's been so hard to consistently, joyfully and effortlessly speak publicly, even though I rock at speaking!) I can literally feel my brain rewiring and energy shifting with this awareness and transformation.

What I just described is what I do for people. I "am" an eternal and loving presence. I invoke my and my client's Divine Guides, and in that space, my clients become aware of memories they haven't had for a long time, or maybe ever. Sometimes bringing memories to light allows them to realize that memories have been "life" instead of life being life. Sometimes the energy shifts immediately. Sometimes, it creates an opportunity to inquire deeper. Clients leave more aware, spacious, empowered and able to Be the Love that They Are!

You may be asking, what does any of this have to do with being a leader?

"Do you ever get stuck in a pattern? Do you ever stop yourself from moving forward?" When you get stuck in a pattern, do you stop yourself and become aware of your thoughts and feelings? I do. That's my life, ongoing awareness. I am committed to an awareness path.

Awareness is transformation. Awareness is my game. The game I was taught. The game that I play. The game that I teach. The game I know like the back of my hand.

"There I go getting nervous about being an example of transformation again."

As I write I can feel the block come up. I witness it. I take a deep breath. I sink into where the energy shifted from open to dense. I pay attention to who I am being. That is life for me. I don't believe in force. I don't believe in pushing through. I don't believe in figuring it out. I believe in love as force. I believe in motion and when I have awareness of love as force, ego pops up. An energetic block is present. My body starts to tense up, and I feel my energy field closing down, like " I" am getting small. I take a deep breath, be, and then a memory comes to me.

In this moment, the thought that comes to the present is, "My mom wants me to die." I get scared at the thought of getting present with that memory, and, because I am courageous, because I am a leader, I stop. I put the pencil down. I get still. I take a deep breath. I sit up straight. I put my hands on my thighs, and I direct my mind to why I am scared. The thought that comes to me is, "Transformation is dying to harm." Transformation means knowing my ego is a rig. It means surviving my tears and scariest moments that aren't real in the first place. It means taking a stand for who I am – LOVE. It means discovering me, prior to and senior to any pain I have ever had. As I see and write these words, the energy in my head starts to move and the room gets brighter.

Being a transformational leader is living like that. Walking your talk. Not knowing what to do until the moment you know what to do. It's not about thinking ahead or having it all figured out. It's about being and doing. It's about trusting more than knowing. It's about being willing to make a mistake. It's about being human. It's about being me.

Being a transformational leader requires faith in the unknown. It requires observation of what is, even if you don't like it. Transformation isn't about getting anywhere or finding results. It's about being and becoming. That's what I do. That's my field of expertise. I help people be more of who they are. I help them transform what doesn't work. I help them become more masterful in their lives, so they get better results.

This story was channeled through me. This is the story my Guides wanted to tell. I didn't have a preplanned agenda for what to accomplish, except to let love, Spirit, I Am work through me. That's what my work is like, and we provide amazing results. We help people transform past lives in seconds. We support the inner child to break free of his/her blind spots that keep you locked down, envious of other people, or plain out mad that your life isn't what you wanted, within minutes. Transformation doesn't have to be hard and it works. "Being" in transformation is life unfolding moment to moment, and transformation allows you to "be here now." Leading from that space makes it easier for everyone.

Being a transformational leader is about infinite reality first and goals in alignment with purpose second. A servant leadership tool I was taught by Dr. David Kamnitzer is to start with a positive purpose that is aligned with your joy. Knowing and aligning with your positive purpose supports you to be grounded in into infinity and prioritize when . . . things happen. When you get off track. When you don't want to do something. When you have conflicting priorities and deadlines.

Most people go back to memory and rely on that for what to do next, or they imagine what it will feel like if they don't get it done. All of that is the mind. Minds can lead you astray. Why, you say? Because the heart field of intelligence resonates differently than the mind. The mind is 3D. It works in facts, objects and states of consciousness like thinking, observing, being, accepting and love like they are objects, that line up next to each other and look the same, and feel the same, unless something feels bad. So, you "are" avoiding feeling bad as a way of setting priorities, unless you have a higher cause, a positive purpose, motivating you and moving you forward. Purpose is that motivator.

Purpose is a sense of knowing that is a soul-driven reason for life. Purpose is the drive that moves me forward when things get bad. Purpose is an activator to consciousness. Purpose IS inspiration. Purpose is beyond reason, so the reasons don't matter. A purposeful being is motivated by love. Purpose is how to motivate yourself beyond the reasons. When you know your purpose, that is fuel. That is drive. That is power. That is what gets people out of bed in the morning and moving when you don't know what to do. Purpose is not a "thing" you think about, find or figure out. It's the essence for which you live. It's the connection to True Self that allows itself to be known when you show up as a heart-based leader. Purpose is undeniably the most important thing I can give share with you in this chapter. KNOW and ALIGN with YOUR POSITIVE PURPOSE!

Going back to why the mind gets you off track. Sometimes when you set out to do something, you receive information. The information itself has no meaning. It's the "meaning making machine" in you that filters and synthesizes what it means. What if seeing life through the filters of a meaning making machine is optional? Step inside that question like a possibility. Say it to yourself out loud and with curiosity. "What if seeing life through the filters of a meaning making machine IS optional?" After you have consciously stepped INSIDE that question, like a possibility, not like you are looking for any particular answer, ask yourself, "What do I see... feel... think... expect to happen... sense... experience in my heart... know to be true from here?" That is transformation. Seeing something new that has always been there, you just simply didn't see it.

Here goes my experience again!! After I wrote that sentence, I started to feel nervous. I am having nervous feelings in my stomach, and the thought that is accompanying those nervous feelings is, "Oh no! What if they found me out?" After I became present to that thought, nervous feelings are still there, although not as intense. Now my lower belly wants to say something: "I am already born again. Why did you die to me so long ago? ("Me" being my intuition.) My stomach is talking. It's having big feelings, like digestion going on and the energy field from my uterus is expanding. I see an energy bubble expand from my uterus area, as if there was a child inside my pants blowing bubbles with a BIG bubble wand. My body jerks as this expanded energy moves through my body. My entire chest starts to shake forward and backward, like when someone is having a seizure. I am having a kriya. The experience of allowing the Divine to work through me in unexpected and unforetold ways is energy expanding, and the new energy is bumping up against the belief system, "I am not enough," which is programing from another lifetime.

Do you know how many people "are" I am not enough as the filter they see life through, without even knowing it?

My business creates the space for these false identities and belief systems to be seen and forgiven, so you "are" enough leading others.

Now the energy in my uterus is moving again. A picture is coming to me, but the picture doesn't present itself. (Maybe because it's impossible to be present with a memory at the same time you are channeling higher dimension consciousness, listening to your body, being present and writing down everything that is happening at one time.) A thought comes to me in the picture's place.

"You can't birth a baby right now; you don't have enough money."

I ask the question, "Is this my thought?"

I hear, "Nope, you are holding and carrying your mother's energy. It was her thought."

I think to myself. "NO WONDER, I have been being "I need money" my entire life.

The energy in my uterus calms and relaxes. The cells and tissues literally start to spread out! I can feel myself energetically sitting more deeply in my body and w-i-d-e-r than I was before this memory and being with this memory came to me. I get a tenseness in my forehead. A memory is coming forward. "Babies don't belong to me." I see a picture of an Aztec structure in my third eye. I hear, "Ladies in bodies are a fear-based system you have been living through. Ladies don't get to have babies in my camp." I see a picture of an Aztec God (male figure). I hear, "You will fight for the rest of your existence if I have anything to do with it."

I take a deep breath and look into the distance. I think to myself, "No wonder it's been so hard for me to birth a project. It has been forbidden unless I wanted to fight. As a peacekeeper, I would never want to fight my way through, so I have been honoring my joy by staying off the planning field, until now." The energy of my body starts to shift again. I felt a pop around my forehead, like a silent and delicate firecracker blew up a belief system that was no longer necessary.

What does any of this have to do with being a leader?

What I just described to you is the water we swim in. It's the water we breathe in. If we avoid it, if we push through it, if we are ignorant to it, if we pretend it doesn't exist, we are missing the opportunity that leadership can be.

Leading people requires us to be present with what is and not make up anything about what is present. Leadership is an art, a science, a transformation and a calling. Not everybody is up for the job. Not everyone is meant to lead me . . . or you.

Here are some of my transformational leadership principles:

Step into the shoes of your follower when you lead.

Be the example you want others to be for you.

Let people know you care.

Be an example you would want to follow.

Be alert so you don't get caught in the should, shouldn't game.

Be a light filled being.

Think more about your follower than you do yourself.

Set yourself up for success.

Don't take on more than you can chew.

These are principles that I was taught and follow, and I hope they support you on your leadership journey.

If this story inspired you, moved you, made you think more about truth, transformation, or leadership, I'd love to connect with you. My best contact information is at www.MaurineXavier.com. If you rejected anything I said, good for you! Your opinion is important to me. I'd love to hear from you too.

Leaders accept both sides of the story the same. Leader's honor and accept opinions without taking them personally or making opinions into more than they really are: another person's point of view.

Here's to Being and Expressing the Love that You Are . . . into infinity and beyond, which is where YOU really ARE!

Maurine Xavier

Maurine Xavier is a recovering CPA who now is a Breakthrough Mentor, Inspirational Speaker and Divine Guide.

Maurine supports women who are here to make a Real Difference and find themselves thinking.

Am I on the Right Path?

I thought I'd be further along by now.

I want more clarity, confidence, and money, but I don't know how!

Women who work with Maurine feel lighter, clear and more confident. They effortlessly start attracting their ideal clients, colleagues and partners. They have increased their earnings from 25% - 300% and become more in the flow with money and abundance. They often start feeling Truly Free for the first time!

Maurine has three decades of experience as a CPA, a financial executive and a wellness entrepreneur. She also has two decades of experience and training in personal growth, healing channeling divine guidance and transformation.

Maurine facilitates Awareness, Healing and Breakthroughs for women online, individually and in groups. She hosts and participates in online workshops and community events. Maurine is also available to speak at Women's Empowerment Summits and Personal Development focused events. *https://www.maurinexavier.com/services*

Maurine spoke at the 2019 Women's Economic Empowerment Global Live event, co-sponsored by Microsoft and the United Nations, and at the 2020 & 2021 Legendary Women of Influence Forums.

Maurine has been married for 33 years and has two children, ages 28 and 26. One of her guilty pleasures is a Philtered Soul with almond milk from Philz Coffee in the San Francisco Bay Area.

Email **maurinexavier@gmail.com**
Phone Number: 650-280-4378
Website: **www.maurinexavier.com**
Facebook page(s):
Personal: **https://www.facebook.com/maurinex**
Business page: **https://www.facebook.com/beaconoflightsolutions**
LinkedIn: **http://linkedin.com/in/maurinexavier**
YouTube Channel:
https://www.youtube.com/user/MaurineXavierSocial media

THE COURAGE OF A LEADER: UNLEASH THE GOLD IN YOURSELF AND YOUR TEAM FOR ULTIMATE PERFORMANCE

AMY RILEY

There is leadership gold inside each of us, whether it's the ability to set an inspiring vision, bring compassion to everyday life, assemble and engage teams, innovate, articulate, collaborate, solve problems or something else. Great leadership is within all of us. It's the gold within us. There is a strength and value that every individual uniquely provides.

As leaders we can support, coach and empower those around us to unleash the gold in themselves.

I've had the opportunity over the past two and a half decades to work with leaders in a variety of industries and at all levels. Throughout that work, I've had moments in which I've been greatly inspired and impressed by leaders. In every one of those moments, the leader was exhibiting courage and putting his/her unique talents to good use.

I've been surprised to notice people saying I have a unique ability to bring out the hidden—or yet unseen gold—in leaders. Clients and business partners have said that I have "the Midas touch."

My initial reaction to these comments is that the leaders do the work! Yet, at a closer look, there are specific techniques that I employ to bring out the true and full potential of others.

Let's look at the 4 secrets to unleash the gold within you and your team.

Secret #1: Leverage Strengths

You want to leverage the strengths of each individual on your team and the talents of the team collectively. The Gallup organization reported in 2019 that employees who learn to use their strengths are 7.8% more productive. Then, when you get the whole team strongly agreeing that they get to use their strengths every day, the team is 38% more productive and their customers (internal or external) are 44% more likely to give high satisfaction scores.

When you get people involved in the work that uses their talents and interests and energizes them, you get the very best of people. The strength work and autonomy has them digging in, being resourceful and feeling more energized and resilient. They get to provide great value in the ways that make sense to them.

The Gallup research statistics refer to the whole team strongly agreeing that they get to use their strengths *every day*. Every day might sound unattainable. Here's how you can get there. First you need to know your team members' strengths. You can use the Strength Exercise on The Courage of a Leader website: http://courageofaleader.com/KnowYourStrengths/. Alternatively, you can simply ask each team member: With what activities do you think you provide the most value? What activities do you enjoy the most? You want to focus in on the activities that each individual does well AND enjoys.

Additionally, you want to understand what unique value your collective team, division or organization provides. What technical skills and what leadership and interpersonal skills set you apart? Go beyond, "We're the marketing team, so we have marketing and promotion skills." What makes your marketing skills noteworthy? Are you really great at capturing complex messages in a powerful and simple way? Do you have a large number of strong relationships in media outlets? Are you masterful at long-term partnerships? Are you known for executing right to timeline? Are you easy and fun to work with? **What is your secret sauce?**

Go after the work that's tailored for your secret sauce. How can you do more of what you do best? Ask your senior leaders this. Ask industry experts this.

Secret #2: Be Flexible

Leaders in my development programs have heard, "Flexibility forwards action, rigidity creates resistance." You want to be flexible and not only allow, yet encourage, team members to decide how the work gets done and how exactly they'll arrive at the intended outcomes. If you get too rigid about how things must go, you'll get resistance, and you won't get creativity, true engagement and people's best ideas.

Yet, it's not flexibility in all aspects of the work at all times. Once you have a Compelling Purpose (vision) and Clear Finish Line (shared goal), you don't want to be flexibly shifting that all the time. That's going to cause confusion and a lack of motivation as team members wonder, "How is the finish line going to be redefined tomorrow?"

You do want to be flexible AS you're defining and fine-tuning the Compelling Purpose and Clear Finish Line. You want to involve others and have their input and insights collectively alter what you're creating. Then, once you've decided the creation process is complete, the Compelling Purpose and Clear Finish Line remain stable. They are your constant North Star, guiding the work and effort.

The flexibility moves through the process. First, you're being flexible as you're working with others to define the *why* (Compelling Purpose) and the *what* (Clear Finish Line) and the *by when* you'll cross that finish line. As colleagues work towards the *what*, you're being flexible about the *how*: how they approach the work, how they define milestones, how they engage others, who they involve, how they format the documents, and so on.

You might now be thinking about the circumstances in which you can't be flexible on the how. There are certainly some! Legalities and safety procedures are the first examples that come to mind. For any procedures or processes that you wish to standardize for safety, for consistent customer experience and/or to create efficiencies, you want to involve a diverse group of employees with different perspectives in the work of defining the standard approach. You're flexible while defining the process. You can, from then on, communicate who was involved in creating the procedure because at some point a new hire is going to encounter procedures that he didn't have a part in creating. Yet, he can learn that many of his colleagues did. And know that he'll be involved in the next standardization effort.

There are always aspects of the work around which you can be flexible. It's just not all aspects at all times. And you want to be really explicit with team members about this, about where there's flexibility and where there isn't. Let employees know what you expect of them, where they have guardrails, and where you want them to flex their creativity. If you feel you're "being flexible" as a leader, yet team members don't know where that flexibility lies, it doesn't do much good and could create confusion and demotivation—the exact opposite of what you were intending to create.

I see too many leaders erring on the side of too much rigidity, thinking the work needs to be done in the way that the leader has been envisioning it. **If we don't allow team members to do their own thinking and apply their strengths in their own way, then we don't get the collective best ideas nor the best value and energy from the team. Instead, we get resistance.**

Secret #3: Engage People's Hearts

70% of engagement is attributed to the leader, according to Gallup (*Randall Beck and Jim Harter, Gallup Business Journal, April 21, 2015*). As a leader, you are the biggest factor in determining whether those around you are fully dedicated and bringing their best to the work, or not.

To get the highest levels of engagement, you need to involve people's hearts and have them feel emotion and passion about what they're involved in. It proves challenging to many leaders, yet there's a single endeavor to focus on: show vulnerability.

Showing vulnerability increases engagement. It's important to show vulnerability with purpose and intentionality. It's not about showing up one day to the office and sharing your most embarrassing childhood moments and most recent family dramas with anyone who will listen. Instead, it's about saying when you've made a mistake, sharing what you know and don't know, asking for others' input and help, trusting others and being willing to share about when you are or have been worried or afraid.

Let's take a look at how you are currently showing your vulnerability. Rate yourself 1 to 10 on the following common vulnerability behaviors:

Say what you don't know

Say where you need help

Be transparent

Ask and allow others to contribute

Change your mind

Trust others to lead

Admit mistakes

Share about yourself

Trust others with key deliverables

Tell others how you're feeling

Choose 1 behavior to play with, amp up and/or do more often. I'd suggest picking the item you rated the highest. This will be the fastest route to strengthening engagement.

Finally, write down specific ideas about how to further engage in this way to show vulnerability.

Secret #4: Check Your Beliefs to Fuel Action

People can tell when they are being fed a line. We know when the person across from us is doing all of the right things yet doesn't believe in what she's doing. When actions are not sincere, we can feel it.

There's a well-known quote from Peter Drucker: "Culture eats strategy for breakfast." You know this one? I don't think this could be more true. I believe similarly that, "Belief eats behavior for breakfast." Having the appropriate beliefs, or outlook, is way more important than perfectly executing the seemingly appropriate behaviors.

If you want to help a person improve and unleash the gold within, you want to believe some of the following about the individual.

is intelligent

is capable

knows how to solve problems

is responsible for own choices

is personally accountable

is creative

has a unique dream/vision or goal

has strengths, talents and skills

knows how to learn

is a whole and complete person

knows how to be clear

has own values and principles

Why? Why do you need to make at least some of these assumptions? So you can be a courageous leader who trusts the capabilities of those around you and coaches whenever possible.

Coaches ask questions more than they tell information. WITHOUT a coaching perspective, you get . . .

. . . NO new ideas or perspectives

. . . NO increased levels of engagement

. . . LIMITED performance

Coaches empower, encourage critical thinking, and thus enable team members to find their own best ideas to improve and achieve the desired results.

Now you know the 4 secrets to unleash the gold within!

What will you do to practice these secrets? Here are my top suggestions for each:

Secret #1: Leverage Strengths

- Ask a team member: With what activities do you think you provide the most value? What activities energize you the most?
- Consider how you can leverage your strengths more.

Secret #2: Be Flexible

- Consider a current project or initiative and ask yourself: What's already defined, around which there's little to no flexibility? Where can you be flexible? Where can others have influence over the how?

- Reflect at the end of the day. Where could I have been more flexible today?

Secret #3: Engage People's Hearts

- Ask someone for help.
- Share your thoughts and feelings on an important issue or aspect of the work.

Secret #4: Check Your Beliefs to Fuel Action

- Complete the Get into the Mindset Guaranteed to Accelerate Trust activity found here: http://courageofaleader.com/mindsetguaranteedtoacceleratetrust/
- Have a coaching conversation in which you focus on asking more than telling.

What are the first actions you will take?

Our world right now needs leaders who are fully stepping into their courage and full potential. You can empower those around you to step in and step up. You have everything you need to practice the 4 secrets and support your team and all those around you to unleash the gold within. Make this kind of difference in our world. You too can have the Midas touch because you've got The Courage of a Leader.

Amy Riley

Amy L. Riley has over two decades of experience coaching executives, developing leaders at all levels and consulting with Fortune-100 companies such as Allstate, Boeing and Cisco Systems. She has worked one on one with hundreds of leaders and thousands more as part of a group to fully step into their leadership, create amazing teams and achieve extraordinary results.

As an international keynote speaker, #1 international best-selling author and top leadership development consultant and coach, Amy knows that every leader produces the most extraordinary results when they leverage their unique strengths and individual leadership style and commit themselves to a personally inspiring leadership legacy.

Amy's most popular keynote speeches are:

- **The Courage of a Leader®:** *How to Inspire, Engage and Get Extraordinary Results*
- **The Courage of a Leader®:** *Create a Competitive Advantage with Sustainable, Results-Producing Cross-System Collaboration*
- **The Courage of a Leader®:** *The Power of a Leadership Legacy*
- **The Courage of a Leader®:** *How to Lead, Sell and Succeed Virtually*

Amy and her husband, Kevin, live in Chicago with their two children, McKenzie and Jake. Amy enjoys spending time with her family and training for running races and triathlons.

If you want your team to have The Courage of a Leader®, grow your collective influence and achieve extraordinary results, contact Amy for a free consultative call. You'll walk away with the top 3 approaches to fulfill your vision for your team. You can schedule your consultative call through The Courage of a Leader® website at www.courageofaleader.com.

amy@courageofaleader.com
773-919-3055
www.courageofaleader.com
https://www.linkedin.com/company/courage-of-a-leader/
https://www.youtube.com/channel/UCCXIynEP0yvY3rEkUKOSYww

Part 3: AUTHENTIC LEADERSHIP

STRONG LEADERSHIP STARTS WITH BEING GENTLE

ARLISS DUDLEY-CASH

Imagine creating your version of a strong leader through self-love.

At the age of 28 years old, I sat on the crinkly papered exam table in a doctor's office in Iowa City. A doctor sat in front of me, with pity in his eyes. He said to me, "You have a rare genetic condition called Ehlers Danlos Syndrome that causes the creation of a mutated form of connective tissue, and you have connective tissue throughout your entire body. I will be surprised if you live past the age of 30. There is no cure."

"There Is No Cure."

I realized that I had accepted the societal norm of overworking myself, using negative motivation and self-hate to establish myself as a leader and I had almost worked and pushed myself to death. Not only that, I also expected the people that I worked with to do that very same thing at the cost of their mental, emotional and physical health. I knew in that moment that I had to make a change within myself to save my own life and change the way that I showed up as a new kind of leader. To model a gentler and more loving way to reach the same level of personal and professional success.

I believe we are trained from an early age to use negative motivation to achieve goals and to lead others. One of the most common forms of negative motivation is through fear and threats. When we are young, we are told that if we do not clean our room or do our chores, we will lose our allowance or a special toy. As we age, this threatening tactic is applied to the loss of promotions or pay if performance expectations are not met. Through this negative motivation, we suffer, hindering our ability to succeed and lead in meaningful ways. The more we are exposed to the use of negative motivation as a norm in leadership, the more likely we are to employ it as part of our personal leadership style. How do we each release the use of negative motivation? **This is done by loving ourselves**.

Based on research done at the Queens University in Canada, we each have over 6,000 thoughts a day. In most people, 80% of these thoughts are negative. We are all connected through energy, and the energy we put forth through our thoughts and words go out before us and contribute to creating the reality that we experience. Our thoughts and words go into the collective consciousness to create the reality we all experience. If we are mean to ourselves, we are contributing to that negative reality as well. Unfortunately, through negative self-talk in the form of criticism, shame and blame, we are creating a consciousness that abuse is acceptable. We are normalizing abuse from the person we are supposed to love and trust the most, ourselves.

I know that this can be extremely hard to hear and cause a physical reaction of recoil, but think about it. Have you ever been in a leadership role and outwardly criticized the work of the employee or individual you were supervising? Most people will say, "Yes," because this is considered the norm in our society. You are probably asking yourself, "Is there is another way to inspire growth and change in individuals as a leader?"

Well, I am here to tell you that there is, and it all starts with you, as a leader, loving yourself.

Once we have normalized abuse from ourselves, we are far more likely to use criticism, shame and blame as a part of our leadership style with others because it is our norm. This means that if we put out into the collective consciousness positive self-talk, self-love, self-acceptance and trust in ourselves as the norm, we are creating a consciousness that self-love and gentleness is okay. We have normalized love and trust from the most important and constant companion we will ever have, ourselves. This affords us the option to show up in our leadership role from a place of love and compassion. Compassion is the ability to have true care for others and make decisions with positive intentions. Compassion in leadership creates stronger bonds between people and creates a sense of loyalty and belonging. This, in turn, can increase morale, trust and collaboration within a group. Imagine leading from a place of compassion and inspiring loyalty, trust and collaboration in your team. Strong compassionate leadership starts from a place of self-love and grows to nurture and foster strong communities.

What does science have to say about this? Nobel prize winner Dr. Elisabeth Blackburn showed that negative self-talk is interpreted by our physical cells as stress and results in the ends of our DNA, the telomeres, being worn down. This is important because the telomeres, which are compound structures that are found at the ends of chromosomes, are needed for the prevention of illness and aging. Our cells are listening to the way we talk to ourselves, and if it is negative, they choose to lessen our ability to stay healthy and live a long life. We know that a characteristic of a strong leader is health, vitality and zest for life. Science has shown that when we talk to ourselves in positive, kind and loving ways, our cells hear those positive words too and interpret that message in a way that preserves the telomeres, supporting us in living longer and heathier lives. As a leader, not only will choosing positive self-talk support you in your own health and vitality, this positive practice will also inspire those you lead to do the same. Imagine having a team of healthy, vital individuals expressing positivity as a core value who thrive under your leadership. **This starts with you and choosing to talk to yourself in loving and supportive ways.**

The most compelling scientific evidence to embrace self-love as a means of becoming a strong and effective leader comes from Dartmouth College. Researchers at Dartmouth College identified the Frontostriatal Pathway as the area in the brain responsible for self-love and self-esteem (Chavez, R. et al, 2015). When this pathway is thick, strong and highly active, individuals experience strong feelings of self-love and self-acceptance. When we choose to show love to ourselves and practice self-care, these loving actions cause the Frontostriatal Pathway to become thicker, stronger and more highly active. This is important because the Frontostriatal Pathway is the bridge between the Prefrontal Cortex (the home of knowledge of self) and the Ventral Striatum (the home of our motivation and rewards system). This research has shown the more we express self-love, we are more motivated and we are more likely to reward ourselves for our achievements. High motivation is a key characteristic of a strong leader. A highly motivated leader is more likely to inspire others, understand what motivates others, reward their team members for their achievements, and more likely to have a team which achieves their goals. There is a strong correlation between the motivation level of the leader and the overall success of the team. Imagine yourself feeling highly motivated and inspiring motivation and achievement of goals in your team. **This all starts with you strengthening and activating your Frontostriatal Pathway through acts of self-love and self-care.**

Imagine what a world would look like if, in the collective consciousness of leaders, there was a strongly held belief that love, trust, inclusivity and authenticity were the choice.

Now that is a world I want to live in! And it all starts with Leaders like you!

We all came into this world, knowing that we are divinely connected to source energy, knowing that we are divinely connected to every living life form in the universe, knowing that we unconditionally love ourselves and every being in the universe. We don't have to learn something new from scratch, it is already in each one of us. We just have to start today by practicing self-love, self-acceptance, self-care and compassion.

The practice of self-love is not always easy, but you can choose to keep it simple.

What can you do to begin to practice self-love every day? You can stand in front of a mirror and tell yourself, "I love you." You can sing yourself love songs, write yourself love notes or give yourself a hug each day. Or you can choose to just start noticing when negativity is present. Listen to the way that you speak to yourself. Is it from a place of gentle loving kindness? If not, with gentle awareness notice when negative self-talk happens without judgment. Just that step alone is a step toward self-love. Be compassionate toward yourself when you view an action, thought or comment as a mistake. The more you practice compassion with yourself, the more likely you are to use compassion when leading others. Finally, schedule time in each of your days to practice self-care. Find a form of self-care that feels right to you. I love to meditate first thing in the morning. Maybe you enjoy sitting and watching the sunset. Self-care is what feels nourishing, supportive and feels good to you. By scheduling self-care you are also strengthening your Frontostriatal Pathway, which will increase your motivation and allow you to more effectively motivate those you lead.

I invite you to **reframe** your mindset, **rebuild** your self-love and **reconnect** to the unconditional love we have all known as our **TRUTH** since our existence. These are the essentials to becoming the strong leader you desire to be.

Self-Love Leadership Tips:

1. Become mindful of your thoughts through neutral curiosity. Notice the thoughts that you have, particularly about yourself, throughout your day. Try not to judge your thoughts as good or bad just begin to become aware. When a negative thought arises consider what a positive thought might be and practice introducing them in a gentle way.

2. Practice speaking positively to yourself. If comfortable, stand in front of a mirror and say out loud positive phrases such as, "Your best is always good enough," "I love you," and "I act in ways to support my happiness and health." This will support your cells and create a more positive mindset.

3. Practice self-compassion by accepting yourself as you are in this moment. Self-acceptance is a nonjudgmental embracing of who you are today. Celebrate the amazingness of who you are. There is always growth and change to be made and that growth is more accessible by starting with gratitude for who and where you are now. Practice self-acceptance through a daily gratitude practice of listing three things each day you are grateful for starting from within.

Can you now imagine loving yourself to being a strong Leader?

Arliss Dudley-Cash

#1 International Best-Selling Author, Business Consultant, and Self Love Coach Arliss Dudley-Cash is an inspirational speaker and self-love movement leader. With a background in business, neuroscience and forensics, her career expands over several industries including operations management, research scientist and death investigation. Arliss unites this eclectic background with her personal journey to overcome the odds and survive a terminal diagnosis. Her award winning presentations include topics on extreme self-love and body positivity. Arliss is a big believer in the magic of our individual stories and the power of storytelling to affect positive change in this world. In 2021, she co-founded The Body Positivity Podcast which she hosts with her friend Diana Gremillion. Through her company Soullutions LLC, she is passionate about helping her clients to become powerful, joyful, authentic business owners experiencing freedom, having a lot more fun in their business, and experiencing the success of their dreams. In her free time, you can find her in the Pacific Ocean, painting or playing with her three chihuahuas—Tonks, Moony and Fluffy on the beautiful Big Island of Hawaii with her partner Matthew. Arliss's dream is for each of us to become the loves of our lives!

www.soullutions.com
Instagram: **@soul_utions** & **@bodypositivitypodcast**
Facebook: Soullutions Consulting & The Body Positivity Podcast
LinkedIn: Arliss Dudley-Cash & Soullutions
arliss@soullutions.com
(808) 990-7685

STAND IN YOUR TRUTH
MARY DESPE

We live in a society obsessed with superlatives.

This is something I know well. Having hired professionals for Fortune 500 companies, technology start-ups, and scrappy Mom-and-Pop small businesses throughout the globe over the past two decades, I can sense if a person is "special." And by "special," I mean that I know when someone is going places—they impact and affect people in ways much greater than your average individual, and typically, they do it for the better.

There never seems to be an end to the advice on how to be seen as one of these people.

To get ahead professionally, for example, we're supposed to impress. We bring up the awards we've won, the accomplishments that dazzle and astound, as well as freely share the instances where we've single-handedly made a pivotal difference in the fate of a company or project . . . all, of course, while appearing extremely humble, kind, funny and many other flattering qualities.

We also associate that same high level of achievement with those who lead. Leaders are the people who have moved up the corporate ladder or in their communities by way of promotion, achieving impressive accomplishments on the job or having graduated with honors from well-respected institutions. In addition, they are, as many believe, gifted public speakers. They immediately attract our attention and fire us up, inspiring those around them with skillful, impassioned messages. They motivate the masses to do more and to be better than ever before. Quite often, they share stories from their past that speak of overcoming incredible odds or extraordinary circumstances. In short, leaders are the people to whom others look up to for whatever they feel they might be lacking during times of crisis and need. Leaders become the voice for those in search of inspiration, hope and at times, bravery.

To be seen by others in this light was something I had always craved, from a young age. I wanted to be powerful and affect people in the way that a leader did. I wanted to have that same attention and admiration everyone bestowed upon them.

Growing up, I remember believing that I could be this person. Why not? After all, my youth afforded me many advantages that would suggest it could be possible. I had the constant support of both of my parents and the companionship of my built-in best friends by way of my four siblings. I was raised in a household where I was lucky to never go hungry, always having fresh and clean clothing on me (even if they were hand-me-downs from my older sister) and a warm bed to sleep in every night. But, like many young people, I was blind to seeing these as blessings, assuming that everyone had these things, too.I often took my parents' attention for granted, viewing their active involvement in every aspect of my life more as an annoyance than something that contributed to my overall well-being and development.

Many Saturdays were spent with my dad tutoring me on concepts that I had difficulty grasping with my algebra homework or with my mom helping me get over my tremendous fear of public speaking by practicing my delivery of an oral book report for class. It was abundantly clear that education would play a significant role in my future success and that performing well in this arena would be the way that I would become a leader. After all, education was the key to, as my parents put it, "everything you'll ever need" in life. With that mindset, I was pushed to excel in school. Through the privilege of education, I performed well throughout every level of school. When I graduated from university with a bachelor's degree and with a master's degree in business, I felt that I was on my way of becoming that successful person I had always wanted to be.

Though I had done well in the classroom, the world would hint that there was much more to creating success that I hadn't quite learned. It would require far more than getting good grades or reading things from a book. To be that leader I had always wanted to be, it seemed that there were other important pieces to the puzzle that I hadn't yet learned.

Those pieces would be things I wouldn't learn from my parents. Rather, I took my cues of how to become a leader from an unlikely source—the television.

Yes, that's right—the television. When you grow up in a place where you're part of the only Filipino family in a predominantly all-White town, it was common to look around for the signs that would indicate it was okay to be different. I looked for the encouragement everywhere—in school, at church, with classmates. Sure, I could commiserate with school friends about our favorite teachers, how certain homework problems were too tough or confusing or even that I also felt the same pressures to do well in school. Though I felt that I fit because I was a strong student, I kept getting messages that I still was an outsider. I could never speak as freely and confidently as most of my peers when asked to share impromptu thoughts about readings in my English literature and history classes. I envied others' fluency and ease with oral communication, as I always seemed to struggle to find the right words. Many times, my teachers would quickly move on to the next student to hear if they could "help me out" when I would stumble constructing the words to say. I felt trapped into being typecast as a poor communicator. Despite being a person who was good at "bookish" things, I couldn't be counted on to speak up and articulate things well. I found that this stereotype followed me outside the classroom. At times, I ignored the barrage of comments from people who would question why my parents would opt to speak *Visayan* to each other while around others that only spoke English, or where I was "really" born because they had never known anyone to look like me in the community. I wanted to fight back, saying something hurtful and equally condescending to retort. However, my typical response was to say nothing and to retreat stoically. I would fake as if I didn't hear a word of it, putting on a brave smile on my face while being eaten alive by feelings of helplessness and weakness.

Television helped me escape these emotions. It offered a window to a world of possibility. I could see people who were different, like me, expressing themselves in ways that I hadn't seen before. It was a type of storytelling with which I never had first-hand experience, let alone saw someone who wasn't White share freely and honestly. Television introduced me to a variety of styles and personalities I'd never known. But importantly, the small screen brought life to people who were different from those I knew growing up. While I empathized with stories of immigrants coming to the United States in the 1960s for educational pursuits just as my parents had experienced, I was both surprised and mesmerized by tales that spoke of a resiliency and courage that I had never known anyone to go through.

I realize it may sound a bit silly to say that television inspired me to believe that I could be more than what I was told I could be. Furthermore, I also know it is such a cliche to say that Oprah Winfrey changed my life. However, it is the truth. Growing up in rural Illinois, I was deeply affected to see someone like Oprah sharing her voice and encouraging others to feel confident in being who they were. To watch someone who looked different from the other talk show hosts at the time commanding attention from audiences without apology gave me a glimpse at what courage and purpose could be. It wasn't her impressive acts of gift-giving to lucky audience members attending the taping of the episode, nor was it the fact that millions of people would watch her talk show daily that got my attention. Rather, I was drawn into Oprah's openness about the struggles she had experienced early in her life, and that she had been able to overcome these incredible difficulties. As she shared details of the physical abuse including being raped by a relative at a young age, Oprah's story pierced me. I had never known anyone to share such deep secrets—things that would be embarrassing and humiliating for most—with such bravery and openness. Though I remember the details in her painful story, it was shared in an unplanned, unrehearsed fashion. There never seemed to be a worry to sound perfect. Seeing others in the audience react with raw emotions and with such respect to her experience made me understand the power of her authenticity.

It was in that moment that I realized the power of a unique perspective. Even though I shared a voice that was different from those around me, I started to believe that I mattered, too.

I began to understand that being a leader was much more than being able to achieve. Oprah was that kind of charismatic force. She made an incredible emotional connection with strangers. Though I adored Oprah, I couldn't help but wonder: what was my story? Did I have anything to offer that seemed remotely interesting? I felt a bit silly. My whole life I had been so proud of being at the top of my class and known as an intelligent person. I believed that such accomplishment would guide me to leadership and being that someone that others looked to. But beyond that . . . what else did I offer? Having a compelling story seemed to gain the admiration, respect and attention of others—but what did it mean when you didn't seem to have that kind of experience in your own history?

I struggled with this for many years. Though I had a burning desire to be known as a leader, I felt lost. I didn't know what special talent I offered the world and felt that I would forever stay unseen. However, when I decided to change jobs and pursue a career as a recruiter in 2006, little did I know that experience would alter the course of my life. Not only did it introduce me to my professional purpose, but showed me the five key things that true leaders demonstrate:

- **Look for the silver lining.**

When I decided to switch into the field of recruiting years ago, one of the first companies with whom I interviewed was a very successful executive search firm in the Boston area. Though I knew I would make a great recruiter, the owner of the firm expressed the contrary. "You're smart and personable enough . . . but you're definitely not a recruiter," he said, to my disappointment. "Recruiters are extroverts, very charismatic, and engage with people very easily," he continued. "You, on the other hand, sit back and listen way too much for this job."

Though I recall feeling crushed when I heard his feedback, I recovered within a few minutes, quickly changing my emotion to one of annoyance. Yes, I knew I wasn't the most outgoing person in the room. But I didn't quite understand why he seemed to trash the importance of listening skills—a trait that I believed was quite important to being a successful recruiter. Perhaps it was because he was looking for the next rainmaker for his firm—that is, someone who would attract and persuade prospective companies to engage his organization to recruit for high-profile positions. As his company focused on executive search, a key requirement for recruiting was to show the ability to bring in new clients.

- **Receive feedback and their truth.**

Though it took a bit of time after the interview to fully appreciate his feedback, I took his observations to heart. I could have stayed annoyed, writing his comments off as disrespect to my ability. Rather, I chose to see it more as the chance to get the unfiltered, candid take on the first impression someone with credibility in the field had of me. By being open to the feedback, I learned two extremely valuable things that emerged as key reasons behind my success in this field.

- **Discover where they need to expand their skill or get support and receive it.**

This disappointing interview gave me the push to genuinely work on the area in my professional background that needed development. Because I wanted to succeed in this field, I took the feedback as the kick in the butt to seek out opportunities to improve my salesmanship and business development abilities. Over the next few years, I scooped up as much education as I could on the topic, from reading as many books and articles, attending training workshops and volunteering for the hands-on experiences that would make me step out of my comfort zone and really flex my salesmanship muscle in the workplace. It wasn't easy, nor did it happen overnight. But, it did pay off to put myself in these professional situations where I was uncomfortable. In time, I dramatically improved my skills around business development with this consistent effort, so much that I gained the confidence to start my own recruitment proprietorship that remains successful in achieving six-figure earnings year after year.

- **Bring their talents forward regardless of being in the spotlight or not.**

Though I'm very proud of the strides I've made to improve my salesmanship ability, don't get me wrong—the success I've had as a recruiter isn't because of it.

Just as I knew during my failed interview years ago, my best skills didn't seem to resonate with the interviewer. Instead of accepting the narrow idea that successful recruiters are extroverts and feeling pressure to change who I was, I stuck to my intuition about the things I did well. I knew I'd go very far in this industry because of my ability to listen and to observe others effectively while being able to slice right to the core of what motivates people. It's not easy staying true to a path that others might criticize or poke fun, true leaders view it as just part of the journey as they keep moving forward.

- **Know failures can lead to some of their greatest successes.**

Although there was a time when I believed extreme extroverts with incredible charisma and flawless oratory skills became leaders, I've found the beauty and meaning in my own style. I am a kind, introverted, observant, intelligent and soft-spoken brown person with a nerdy sense of humor . . . and I matter. Not only am I proud of these traits, I offer them as my voice to the world, and it is as powerful a perspective to have as any. True leadership is authentic leadership, and I am proud of how I've made my impact.

Mary Despe

Mary Despe is a Recruitment Consultant and Careers Influencer based on the North Shore of Oahu, Hawaii. She is the Owner of MK Despe Consulting, a recruitment and careers sole proprietorship. For close to 20 years she has connected amazing talent with outstanding start-ups and organizations in North America, Western Europe and Australia. She advises entrepreneurs on how to avoid the "I need to clone myself" and other panicked approaches to hiring, and promotes strategies that align people in productive, successful partnerships. Though she enjoys working with businesses to build high-performing teams, Mary is passionate about helping job seekers attract and land the opportunities they desire. She has coached professionals to secure new roles and navigate industry changes through unique personal brand strategy.

Mary contributes to websites such as Career Addict, Fairygodboss, Medium and LinkedIn, and has been featured in hiring-related articles for Honolulu Civilbeat, Refinery29 and LinkedIn's Get Hired newsletter. She has been a featured speaker at the 2021 Honolulu Women's Leadership Conference and the 2020 and 2021 Women's Leadership & Empowerment Conferences in Bali, Indonesia. She is a regular contributor to Girls Nite Live, an international e-commerce and education platform that empowers and amplifies the voices of women through online programming for women, by women.

LinkedIn: **https://www.linkedin.com/in/mkdespe/**
Facebook: **https://www.facebook.com/mkdespeconsulting**
Instagram: **https://www.instagram.com/marydespe/**
YouTube: **https://www.youtube.com/c/MKDespeConsulting**
Website: **www.marydespe.com**

LEADERSHIP BEGINS WITH WHO YOU ARE
TRACIE ROOT

Being a leader often (usually? always?) means forging your own path and inviting others to join you on your journey. Stand up. Stand in front. Be seen in both success and in struggle. Have perseverance. Resilience. Courage. Take decisive action toward your dreams. Bring people with you. Sounds simple, right?

> *"Our deepest wishes are whispers of our authentic self. We must learn to respect them. We must learn to listen."*
> *—Sarah Ban Breathnach*

My client, Sara, believed people judged her negatively. She believed others thought she didn't know what she was doing. She believed others didn't take her seriously because she has a youthful personality and enjoys directing her fun-loving attitude toward difficult things.

She is not alone; many of us have felt like this. Her perspective is not unique. She told herself that nobody would ask for her help, let alone pay her for it, because she wasn't "serious" enough. Seriously.

Sara felt alone, like she was the only one who saw humor in the hard things. Humor was her unique gift. By finding the funny in the frustrating, she was able to help her clients breathe a sigh of relief, knowing that they were seen, and understood, and that their "problem" wasn't such an obstacle after all. What if humor is the tool they needed to calm their own anxious feelings?

People want JOY. Sara dispenses joy like bubbles from a bubble machine—erratic, floating, iridescent orbs that reflect the smiling faces around her. Like the bubbles, the joy is abundant when we're around her and we can see it all around us.

In turning her thoughts toward what was possible instead of what she already thought was true, she was able to shift, and to lead herself toward a new future where she found amazing clients who loved her and viewed her humor as a superpower rather than a deficit.

"If you obey all the rules, you miss all the fun."
—Katherine Hepburn

Leadership Begins with Who You Are.

People are born leaders. All of us! We need to remember that! We are all bold, unique, creative beings from birth. We explore. We invite others to explore with us. Babies create their own way of communicating. Their own baby language! They didn't learn it, it developed from within as a result of the influences around them. Toddlers create all the time! They bravely stand up and WALK! Imagine never having walked before and deciding to do something you've only seen the kind giants around you do. It would be like us realizing our arms were really wings and jumping off the roof with a flap-flap-flap!

What? You don't want to jump off the roof? Keep reading . . .

"The most courageous act is still to think for yourself. Aloud."
—Coco Chanel

Fear Is Learned. It Can Be Unlearned.

Fear is designed to keep us safe from harm or danger. What danger do we experience in the 21st century? What do we fear? It can be different for each of us.

Let's recap Maslow's Hierarchy of Needs*

- Physiological: air, water, food, shelter, clothing, reproduction
- Safety: personal security, employment, resources, health, prosperity
- Love & Belonging: friendship, intimacy, family, sense of connection
- Esteem/Ego: respect, self-esteem, confidence, status, recognition, strength, freedom
- Self-Actualization: desire to become the most that one can be

A person struggling with health issues may be in fear for their physiological needs. A person who has lost a job may be searching to fulfill their physiological and safety needs. Someone who has dealt with a traumatic relationship may be looking for love and belonging AND the lack of such

* https://en.wikipedia.org/wiki/Maslow%27s_hierarchy_of_needs

may be affecting the adjacent needs as well. At the same time, people who are stable in the first three areas may be looking for status, recognition, self-esteem AND may be concerned at the same time about belonging, appearing ego-centric, and concerned about weakening friendships or a lack of connection with others. Complicated, right?

What is really great about this hierarchy, when we can internalize it, is to see that the "lines" between each "level" are FUZZY! FLUID! We are always moving between the levels and that's *natural*! Personal leadership can include recognizing this for ourselves and leadership of others includes helping them see this truth as well.

One of the best lessons I've learned on this journey to self-actualization is realizing we are not on a straight path from base to peak of this mountain! Rises and falls along the path are completely normal and are NOT a sign of our worth! A rollercoaster of progress or even a *cha-cha-cha* of forward-backward-forward motion is totally normal and even to be expected. We can feel happy even when things are hard, unknown, unfamiliar, uncomfortable—in fact, we can be happy BECAUSE of these things. And, particularly because we've invited others to join us on this path, to share these ideas and these truths with others.

"We can do hard things."
—Glennon Doyle, Untamed

I've Had an "A-ha" Moment.

I have had the incredible opportunity in this past decade to learn from fantastic, successful, inspiring mentors. Some of these people I am blessed to know personally. Others I have seen on stage and on dozens of videos and Zooms, heard them speak, and I know people who know them—we're connected in 2 or more degrees of separation. This morning I realized some of the people I've been following—men and women whose invitations to follow I had accepted years ago—were not leading me to a place I wished to go. I admired them for what they had accomplished. I didn't really know anything about their values. So today, I realized that I want to be on this journey with people whose values I share. I had admired them for what they'd done in their business without knowing much about who they are as people. At our core, we were not aligned.

When our personal and moral values are aligned in all areas, this is a joyful and fulfilling journey. When we follow a path based on limited knowledge, we sometimes hit a bump in the road that helps us recognize the misalignment. I found myself no longer aligned with these people I'd been following—and that is absolutely ok.

I'm not sure if they've changed, but I know I have. Happily.

So, they are happy (I think? I hope?).

And I am happy.

And we are not aligned nor on the same path.

I resist labeling "why" this misalignment occurred because I do not know their true heart, experiences, or reasons for feeling or believing the way they do. And, it doesn't matter. It doesn't feel good to me to follow them any longer, so with no ill-will, I will go another way. I will go in the direction of what feels good to me. I will join those who I am aligned with and we will move on. And that feels good.

Remember Sara? She felt alone and misunderstood. She told herself a story that was untrue and couldn't recognize the positive energy she was bringing to others because she was self-conscious and worried about where she fit in the world. And when she decided to show up authentically and to be open to those around her, to recognize the alignment between her values and those of the people around her, she was able to be joyful and fulfilled and full of gratitude.

"It's good to feel good."
—Gabrielle Bernstein, Super Attractor

And Now I Know.

It took me a while to realize the truth about what I was learning.

As children, we learned to do art before we knew it was art. We took the world as it was and we changed it. We created something new just to see if we would like how it turned out. We ripped things, spread things around, collected things, mashed them together. Finger paint. Play-dough. Stacking things. Knocking them down. Taking things apart. Putting them back together in a new and different way. Nobody told us what to do or how to do it. We made our own choices and we led ourselves to the decisions we made. It came from within. We created and took personal responsibility for our path. We were born leaders, full of personal leadership skills.

Now as an adult and especially as a coach, leadership means I have the ability to direct myself *and* to influence those around me. Personal leadership and the leadership of others. I believe in myself and the choices I make, and I am a role model for the benefit of others. I motivate myself and others toward their goals. I focus on People and Results. This is where the transformation shows up.

Where I started:

- I felt alone.
- I felt helpless.
- I was exhausted.
- I was unable to find fulfillment.
- I saw no future.

- I was closed-off emotionally.
- I was joyless.

And now, each of these has a solution, a skill that takes practice.

- I ask for help.
- I build new healthy habits.
- I practice self-care.
- I discover new things to enjoy.
- I dream big!
- I allow my heart to be open to others.
- I practice gratitude.

When you are struggling with defining yourself as a leader, don't forget Sara and the truth about herself she had to find. Don't forget my list above and my commitment to personal growth and personal responsibility. Don't forget that finding our way is never a straight line and along the way we definitely feel like we're on a roller coaster, or doing a *cha-cha-cha*.

And in the end, the DOing isn't even the thing. I dream, I practice gratitude, I ask for help. These are things I do. But to BE a leader, it's not only to DO these things, but to BE the person who values these things and does the work. I want to BE a dreamer. I want to BE a grateful human. I strive to BE someone who is willing to ask for and accept help. I am not perfect, you are not perfect, nobody is perfect. We are Human BEings, or as a friend said to me, a Human BECOMING. Isn't that beautiful?

"It's not your job to like me, it's mine."
—Byron Katie

How Are You a Human BECOMING?

Look at that list above. Make your own. Take out your pen, take a few deep breaths and write your own list of how you are growing, creating, becoming. Right here in the margins! Who are you becoming? How are you becoming? What will you do differently to become the person of your own future? Where do you fit in the world? It's based not on what we do - but who we are.

BE a Leader. You *Are* a Leader.

Tracie Root

Tracie Root is a coach, a speaker, an educator, and a community builder.

Tracie ended her career in corporate America and found her new calling after a personal family tragedy. Her partner of almost 20 years passed away after a battle with Cancer, at the age of 47. Tracie and her two toddlers were left with no family nearby, a house "underwater" from the housing crisis of 2008, and couldn't see how anything was going to change. Ever.

Then, years later—a spark. That light inside her, dimmed after years of trauma and loss, finally started to shine brighter. She saw a way back to her former self and began the journey, one step at a time. She shifted her career to one of helping others at a deeper level while making more time for her own fulfillment, adventure, and joy.

Now Tracie helps women remember their best selves. For almost a decade, she has been serving and supporting clients around the country to SET and to GET their goals in health, in life, and in business. With the founding of Gather in 2019 and its expansion in 2020, she took her own goal-getting advice and created a community of like-minded women who are growing and thriving together. Tracie serves women around the US in her group programs and in the Gather community to expand their thoughts and dreams to live their BOLD life!

Tracie is an engaging and enthusiastic speaker. Audience members take away the belief that they can do ANYTHING! Tracie speaks frequently on cultivating optimal health and well-being, goal-setting and strategy, entrepreneurship, overcoming tragedy and loss, and other personal development topics.

Tracie lives in Santa Cruz, CA, is married to her best friend, and they are raising two teens and a dog.

Tracie@TracieRoot.com
408-687-0765
Tracie@TracieRoot.com
Tracie@GatherInSantaCruz.com
https://www.facebook.com/tracie.tree.root
https://www.facebook.com/tracieroot.coaching
https://www.facebook.com/gatherinsantacruz
https://www.linkedin.com/in/tracieroot
https://bit.ly/TracieRootYouTube

LEADERSHIP WISDOM
KAI DEERING

Wisdom comes to us in many ways. Sometimes we learn through our circumstances, sometimes through our life experiences, both good and bad, and sometimes from experts that may speak about it or write about it. In my case, I have learned valuable lessons about leadership in each of these ways.

When I was in a corporate sales job, I was confident, headstrong, competitive. I didn't particularly appreciate being told what to do. Mainly because what I was doing was reaping a significant financial reward for the company and myself. I would not say I liked authority, I was not too fond of the rat race, and I didn't like the corporate environment. My boss and I didn't agree completely, and maybe because I was a strong personality, she may have been intimidated by my success. Eventually, she decided to fire me for insubordination. Although it did not make sense, it was a great service to me because it allowed me the time to reflect on what I wanted out of life. I knew there must be more for me than doing the same thing day in and day out.

When it was finally over the difficult situation with my ego-driven boss I realized I needed to be in control of my own destiny and not let any person who had control over my employment dictate my life. For me, the valuable lesson was never to give my future over to anyone else. I knew if I applied all I had learned, I could make my own opportunities, and I would be solely responsible for the decisions I made, both good and bad. I wanted to be in charge of my life and be accountable for my choices and reap the benefit from them. I would make it by doing something I designed that I could control and was based on my efforts. So, I took a year off and researched many business models. One rose to the top of the list.

All I had learned really paid off when I decided to start an insurance brokerage. I was going into the insurance business, and it made sense to me at the time because I was looking for a business that included a way to receive residual income. This was important, but I soon discovered I did not enjoy the business at all. Upon reflection, I had chosen it for the wrong reasons, and I found it unfulfilling and boring. This wasn't what I wanted to do long-term. But it was a steppingstone to what lead me to my next move.

One of the values add- on products we offered at my insurance brokerage was LegalShield. This was also something I took advantage of in the corporate world. When I realized I could narrow down what I would offer to just one product, I decided that was the direction I wanted to take. They say the riches are in the niches, and I have found this to be true.

So, I made one more shift, and it was a much better match for me personally. What I loved was working from home and empowering people with our memberships. It was twofold, a business opportunity for women like me and the product of legal advice and assistance at an affordable price. It made so much sense and was an excellent match for me.

LegalShield is a business I truly could stand behind and have for twenty years now. They also had the philosophy of helping their associates grow into success by exposing them to successful mentors. Our people receive the tools they need to be well-rounded in all aspects of life, not just business. Their conferences are focused on helping people with their independent businesses. You have the flexibility to have a life compared to most corporate jobs that consume your life.

One aspect that I had been able to take advantage of in the corporate setting was learning about and embracing personal development. Being a top producer in the corporate world exposed me to becoming a leader through learning from some of the greats. Having a budget to attend high ticket conferences exposed me to outstanding mentorship and education on leadership to leveraging my time and everything in between.

One thing I love is that we teach our sales associates to build relationships and educate people. We use our fear-proof and skill-proof system because no one likes to be "sold." It is really a "no brainer" to have such a low-cost service that helps people when a need arises for an attorney's advice. In so many ways, it is a business in a box; you do not need to reinvent the wheel. This business model is a win-win-win-win. The client wins, the associates win, the attorneys win, and the corporation wins. Fear is commonly used in the insurance business, and this went against how I wanted to conduct my business. I wanted to serve from my heart. Founded in 1972, they have been helping people and leading in the services they provide for nearly fifty years. I am honored to be a part of it.

Leadership is so important to me. In our business, we have many leaders who are admired and deserve respect for how they lead. Most people believe leaders are born. And although some people have a personality that lends itself to being a leader, leadership is a learned skill. No one is born a leader. I would say that leadership is influence, nothing more or nothing less. And the first person you must lead is yourself. If you can understand these two principles, then you are miles ahead of the pack.

What I loved was the business model. You were not working alone, but with people who wanted the best for you and wanted to help you succeed! Much different from the dog-eat-dog corporate world. Empowering people with our memberships was perfect because I was rewarded for my efforts within the organization. At the same time, I remained in control of what was important to me. Having a business opportunity as we do, offers so much to help to women who need to build sustainable futures. And while they amass a substantial book of business, they have mentors who care about them while they grow.

The women I work with are much like I was when I started. They may be single and want to support themselves because they have discovered the harsh nature of corporate life. They may be married and realized that having children would be frowned upon commonly in the corporate world. In most of these environments, it puts them at a disadvantage if they need time to spend at home. Many don't want someone else raising their kids; they want to be a hands-on parent that can manage their own time and fit their business around motherhood.

Most people fall into a line of work. It may be what their parents do or wanted to do. It might be the "family" business, for example, teachers who encourage their kids to become educators also. They invest in college, get the credential, and start teaching. But what they have always wanted was to be their own boss. Most don't even consider doing what they love. The parents or a spouse often disapprove of the dream they have and talk them out of it. When we create the life we love, we are so much happier, but most focus on how much money they can make right away.

Even though I was good at sales, I didn't like the job. Being an entrepreneur was much more to my liking. It matched my personality, and most of all, I could help people and not compete with them. I look for coachable women, willing to start at the bottom and hungry for success. The women I look for are usually confident, sometimes like healthy competition, and they have the heart to help people. This is possible at LegalShield through philanthropic efforts. The people I work with want to build a team that grows together, and they all want to be more than just average.

If you are ready to build a team and duplicate your efforts, you can do this by becoming a leader in a company that helps you be in your own business. All the heavy lifting has already been done, and you are not trying to figure it all out alone. Another part of learning to be a leader was realizing that a leader's greatest return is to develop more leaders. Because leadership is influence, it is essential to become influential. Influence is earned and doesn't come into your life by accident. It is a series of intentional acts and begins with personal growth.

The question then becomes, how do we grow? I recall many years ago finding out the importance of having a personal growth plan. We can set goals and then make a plan or map out a way to achieve the goals. Here is a great place to begin:

The first part of your map is determining where you are currently, like the little red dot at the mall directory, "You Are Here." You won't get anywhere on a map unless you know where you start. First, assess your skills, experience, and your education. Write these things down. Then, add the things that you love to do. When you look at these areas, they will likely point you in the direction you should go.

Then look at your associations! Jim Rohn famously said that we are the average of the five people we spend the most time with. Look at the people you spend time with. Are they telling you all the reasons you can't do what you want to do, or are they helping you see all the ways you can achieve your goals and, ultimately, your dreams? Look for groups of people with a positive outlook and that are willing to help one another. Are the role models who are already where you want to be? Look for mentors or coaches to give you great advice, then act on it. Stand on someone's shoulders who believes in you until you build the confidence you need to achieve your goals!

Stanford University published a study titled "How We Learn." Their findings revealed that 89% of people are visual learners, 10% are auditory learners, and 1% learn by using their other senses. So, based on these findings, we know leadership is "caught," not taught! When we find leaders that match our values, we can follow their lead as we witness the influence in action! And until we have the confidence, we need to be the leader others want to follow!

Once you know where you are, make sure your mindset is right to go towards your goals. The worst frame of mind is to tell yourself, "I already know that." Look for the ways to do things you need to do. Even if you have heard it before but are not doing it when it makes sense, find out why! Be in a constant state of curiosity. Learn to ask questions when you have time with a mentor, do your homework to ask valuable questions. People love to help people who are eager to learn. Please don't waste your time or theirs; be prepared.

The biggest challenge was trying to apply what I did in the corporate world to the business plan of LegalShield. It didn't work that way. It was about relationships, not about knowledge. My reputation proceeded me in corporate selling, and I lead a group of salespeople. Still, they followed me based on my success and reputation.

Starting with LegalShield, I was beginning the same as everyone starts, at square one! One step at a time I worked my way into a top earner position. I was learning all the way!

The most important thing I have found is to continue to improve myself, and the rest just follows. I needed to get my own ego out of the way because my successes in the past didn't equate to success in the business I was in. It is a people business, and my focus had to be on those I was leading. I was never afraid of hard work, but I started with a clean slate. Everyone starts at the same place; you bring your experience with you, of course, but you need to be open to doing things a certain way, the way that works.

LegalShield is a simple business. Some make it harder than it needs to be. It is about duplication; you don't need to be creative. You do what has been found to work. I found that the people I lead need to be inspired to stay with it; if I keep them inspired, they will stay in the game until they win. It is more than motivation. They need to have self-motivation. I know that quitters never win, so I try to make sure they don't quit. I help them get paid and get connected to the people that will help them along the way, including me. Sometimes I need to help them become confident in themselves and the product. Then, when they grow into that, they can help others do the same, and then they become unstoppable.

Leaders will make mistakes. In most environments, this is detrimental. But as a leader in my business, when you make honest mistakes and are transparent about them, and you and help others with what you've learned from them, they will love you despite any mistakes you make. A leader may do unpopular things, but when they are for the good of the organization and done with the heart, the people understand.

So often, people lead others thinking everyone needs to like them. It is okay if everyone doesn't like you. You can't take it personally! Look for those that you can lead authentically, and let the others go. To reach my goal of being the first woman in LegalShield to make **one million dollars** in revenue a year, I need to continue to grow and lead from the front. For this to happen, I know it is all about serving. My goal is to be the best leader I can be and to help others do the same. I want to be an example of what is possible for women. Women limit their thinking, and they settle sometimes. They join my team thinking this is just a little side hustle. I want them and you to see the potential, which is unlimited. I want you to know that you don›t need to settle for anything short of your dreams.

Leadership Wisdom Tips:

Find what you love, then love what you do.

Continue to grow yourself, especially in the areas of relationships, equipping others, positive attitude and your own leadership skills.

Being a leader is authentically caring about those you lead, being committed to serving them at the highest level possible.

Remember teamwork makes the dream work. Find people to be a part of your team, and the tide of success will lift each of you.

Summarize key point for the reader.

Finding what you love and what you can pour your life into is the first part of leadership. Once you find the dream, find like-minded people to share the dream with you. Care about them, learn about them, and inspire them see the vision and value of the team. Grow in your leadership effectiveness first, then grow your team. Remember your effectiveness needs to be developing continually, then you can lead the people who are following you.

Kai Deering

Kai Deering is an inspirational speaker, contributing author of three best-selling books, philanthropist, millionaire club member, a multiple six figure earner and Network Vice President with LegalShield. She teaches the concepts of winning in your business or career, not from theory but from a life of doing. Want to quit playing small, recapture dreams shelved and learn new ways of being? Kai is a woman entrepreneur and leader to learn from.

Kai has been on the cover of Home Business Connections and Living Well magazines. She has also been featured in Gentry Magazine, Women's Connection Magazine, The Advocate and many other publications. She has appeared on the San Jose television show, Real Estate Weekly and has shared powerful insights on numerous podcasts.

Kai is an ambassador of her local chamber who is also an affiliate marketing partner of hers. Additional professional affiliations include Business Women's Community - Mountain View Facilitator, Business Friends of Silicon Valley - Inaugural member and on the leadership team of her BNI and Polka Dot Powerhouse.

http://ConnectWithKai.com

THE RELUCTANT LEADER

CHWEN LIM

At a certain point in life, I found myself shying away from leadership roles. The more I know about what leadership entails, the more I want to avoid it. Why? I was afraid I might not do a good job. I might not be able to lead well. I thought so much about the result that I forgot about the process of leadership.

Tracing back to my childhood in a Singapore village, I was always the one who suggested games to play and led activities to engage my neighbors, cousins and siblings. We had a make-believe library and other pretend classroom fun. We also toured around our village and explored. Being the eldest in the family, I had to bring my younger siblings with me, and if any of them were injured while we were out playing, I would bear the blame. My parents are understanding parents and they adopted a liberal approach in raising us four kids. However, I still found the burden of being the eldest was not fun. For example, I had to eat more because mom said I was the eldest child; I was the chosen one to accompany my grandma to the market, doctor's appointments, and to visit her friends. Because I was the eldest one, I could take care of grandma.

At age thirty-seven, my pregnant mom, along with my only brother, who was seven years old, were both killed in a fatal car accident in 1977. I was 11 years old and devastated. The court later set the lady driver FREE for no reason. Our family felt the situation was unfair and felt no justice. But we were not strong enough to challenge the authority and demand an answer. I started to question: Where does man come from? Why are we here? Where will we go when we die? Is there someone who leads our life? As a designer, I tend to think, "Who designs our life path?" If we were being designed and placed on earth, we need to know our design objective so we can live up to it. Why would my mom be on earth for only 37 years? She had a happy marriage with four happy children and a warm family. She was a fashion teacher. Did she have to leave this world in such a terrible way? I was in search of a leader in my life.

Looking back, I see the qualities of leadership had already surfaced within me at a young age. In primary school, I hoped my teacher would choose me to be class monitor. It was a special position to serve because the class monitor commanded the class to stand up when a teacher or principal entered the classroom as a sign of respect. They also collected test papers and passed out exercise books, helping the teachers in whatever they needed. But I never got to do that position. Instead, I was chosen to be a prefect. We wore neckties during recess to show our roles, and we were tasked to oversee the discipline of the students. We would do things like ask those who ran to walk and block the entrance to the classroom when everyone should be playing on the playground and not in the classroom. I liked it and felt proud to be a prefect.

In secondary school, I wrote and directed skits for our class, organized BBQs, overnight camps, and planned the meals and activities. I simply enjoyed seeing the joy of those who participated in the activities. One of my extra-curricular activities was National Police Cadet Corps, where we learned to march a squad of 30 people from point A to B by shouting commands so the squad members would follow. I won a few awards for my performance and worked my way up in Junior College to become a Cadet Inspector.

Those were the fun and adventurous days when we had no fear, and we volunteered for everything and anything. Can you believe I was a shy and introverted person? Yes, I was a good team player, but I was not loud and talkative. I would assume any tasks given to me, and I would take it on as my responsibility. A Singaporean journalist once described me as one who "drives in silence" (静中带动)) when she interviewed me for a newspaper about my artwork selected to represent Singapore at a regional young artist contest and about the merit award I won.

Art is what I loved to do and knew I could do well. I quietly did my art with the encouragement of my parents, who were also fond of art. My dad was a renowned artist in Singapore. Seeing him organize and curate exhibitions, edit and publish art catalogs, and hold meetings at home with artists from different countries expanded my view of what art can do. I wished one day I might be able to do the same to influence the art world.

When I know I have the abilities and skills to do something, like art, I know I can be a leader. Likewise, in my career, I was trained in graphic design and graduated with an honors degree from Central Saint Martin School of Art and Design in the UK. The school emphasizes the importance of idea exploration, and students are encouraged to lead the industry with unique styles and embrace technologies to establish a cohesive brand.

When I switched my career to web development years later, the transition was easy because of my comprehensive art school training. I was the creative/art director for my clients. I helped them consolidate their business identities via websites and other collateral. I partnered with maWebCenters® Web Solutions to provide my clients with more services empowering them to control their web presence consistently without obstacles.

When I started looking for a system to scale up my business, like Michael Gerber's book, *The E-Myth Revisited* suggested, it found me. My programmer evaluated the platform and system, and with his blessing, I have been partnering with maWebCenters® since 2005. I am grateful for the responsible partnership I have with the company. maWebCenters® is willing to listen to the needs from the field and they provide updated solutions to help our interconnected businesses grow.

I liked the business model so much that I became a maWebCenters® certified trainer. As a trainer, I was able to teach and share the concept and solutions with many entrepreneurs and industry pros who were looking for a system to partner with. I speak three languages fluently and shared the opportunity with people in Hong Kong, Taiwan, Singapore, and the United Kingdom.

As a trainer, I was given the opportunity to speak about web solutions onstage to 600 people, then 3,000 people, 8,000 people, then 20,000, and then on Zoom, YouTube, and social media to people worldwide. I have received numerous awards and was honored three times as Certified Trainer of The Year in 2009, 2019 and again in 2021. All of this happened because I love using the platform and want more people, be it business owners or graphic/web designers like myself, to know about the system and how it can help them scale up.

During this process, I formed teams in different countries. I am a people person and am very relational. I can make friends easily and help solve individual problems. I love to work with business owners as they always have interesting stories, services and products. I love them as they are the true entrepreneurs who embrace their calling and mission in their business. Business owners' passion always inspires me.

I faced many challenges when I began building and leading my own team. I do not like to order or command people. In my role as an art instructor at a school where students listened to my direction, I felt at ease guiding them, but in a team-building scenario, each participant is an adult with their own goal and mission. Deep in my heart, I do not want to lead. I just want to share web solutions opportunities and watch businesses plug into the system and grow.

When I began to realize that teams need leaders, I hesitated, battling with my inner self. I questioned, why do I need to be a leader? I am happy when I can work by myself and leverage support from web solutions. I just need to work with my clients and get things done. But ever since I started sharing web solution opportunities with those who crossed my path, my team started to grow from local to global.

Leadership, a word that seemed easy and nice to take on in the past, was now heavy. The more team building was mentioned, the more I struggled. I did not want to spoil my relationships, and I did not want to lose friendships. It was stressful. I prayed. I sought help from paid coaches and counselors. I took various personality tests. I started on a journey to find my own identity to discover who I am and how I behave. I was so resistant to leadership that I gave myself many good reasons not to lead.

I read my Bible and found that Moses' father-in-law asked Moses to delegate his judgment to other leaders. I did not have a big team like Moses, but I did have a few teams here and there: an art teaching group, business associate groups in various countries, volunteer groups and networking groups. I had a few task-oriented business partners who were good at organization building. We took different personality tests and discovered what roles we excelled at. I learned to delegate. We were able to embrace our personalities, and once those traits were in place, our team was able to grow.

I tend to worry about the outcome and result of my work and forget to acknowledge myself for the progress my team and I have made. Very often,

I will beat myself up for not being able to achieve results for the team. I heard the producer Dallas Jenkins of the TV show *The Chosen* share a message from one of his fans: "Don't worry about feeding the 5,000, worry about the loaves and fish." Jenkins could not hold his tears as he faced a huge challenge when creating the episodes. He was encouraged by those words. He experienced divine intervention, realizing it is the preparation of himself that is more important than feeding 5,000. I resonate with that as I used to be a perfectionist and am now learning to be more pragmatic without losing aesthetics.

When I read John Maxwell's *How Successful People Lead*, I was impressed by his five levels of leadership: positional > permission >production > people development > pinnacle. I like the way Maxwell simplified the different levels, which emphasized that leadership and respect need to be earned. There is no quick elevator kind of success but a staircase of hard work. I started to understand why the retired people I met at the Rotary Club still display amazing leadership skills in leading the community. When younger generations aim to do less and rest more, successful retirees are quietly working to duplicate their successes to empower younger generations. I think that this is so beautiful.

I have received many blessings from those successful leaders. They have willingly mentored me and coached me along my life path. If I were to write a book, I would like to write about these angels in my life. Their existence helps me tread through many challenging moments. Their encouragement pushes me into leaving my comfort zone and aiming for higher milestones than I could ever reach.

Among all these, the leadership of Jesus is always my best model. The way He led his disciples amazes me. Their personalities were so diversified, and so were their goals and needs. Some were mellow, some were like thunder, some were quick in temper and others were introverts. But Jesus was able to teach and coach them by living with them. Through lifestyle teaching, He reprimanded bad behaviors at the right time. He even demonstrated humility by washing disciples' feet. He led with love and truth, even if He could capture one's heart with authority.

I met God in London during my studies. I willingly surrendered myself and allowed Him to lead my life. Today, I have no regrets. I know I serve a living Savior! My only regret is I should have accepted Him long ago, when I was in third grade. Having a good leader in life is crucial. A good leader will take you where you want to go, but an excellent leader will take you where you do not want to go but ought to go. I am glad I have chosen one, and I still have a few wonderful leaders whom I am following on my life journey.

I like to use "What Would Jesus Do" (WWJD) as my motto for leading my team. When I am confronted with conflict resolution, I will use this acronym to remind me—WWJD? I am still on my journey to learn and grow. I know I will be a better leader when I can be a better learner.

If you are a reluctant leader like me, why not engage a coach or some accountability groups, find a mentor, leave your comfort zone and allow yourself to grow and you will see your breakthrough. Think of the famous movie saying from *The Chosen*, "If not now, when?"

I recently accepted some leadership roles and was so worried I may not be able to handle them. Surprisingly,people around me stepped up to offer their resources. I am so blessed to experience the freedom from breakthrough!

Chwen Lim

Chwen Lim is passionate about graphic design and enjoys coaching small and medium-sized businesses through creating online branding to tell the story of their products and services on the web. Chwen earned her honors degree in Graphic Design from University of the Arts London—Central Saint Martins and her postgraduate teaching diploma from Nanyang Technological University, Singapore.

After Chwen moved to California with her husband and two sons, she continued her education at West Valley College and learned web design. She became a mentor to other students in the program and created a solid network of new friends and business contacts.

In 2007, Chwen joined maWebCenters® and became a Certified WebCenter Trainer. Collaborating with the website building platform helped her provide intuitive website design her clients could easily update independently. Chwen has been recognized for her leadership and training abilities, earning both the WebCenter Trainer of The Year three times and the Webcenter Challenge Award in 2021.

Chwen has traveled extensively throughout Asia for her online business and also to ensure her late artist father's work is professionally curated and documented. She worked closely with museum curators, art gallery owners and collectors to educate future generations on South East Asia art history. Before his passing in 2008, Chwen helped her father put together the giant public mural art piece, "Let the Show Begin" in Singapore's underground Esplande train station.

Painting in the studio with her youth and adult students is a favorite way for Chwen to reconnect with her artist roots. She also conducts annual creative summer programs for children and coaches Sunday school teachers at her church. She is actively involved with community and business networking as a member of organizations like Business Network International (BNI) and Rotary.

Linkedin: **https://www.linkedin.com/in/chwenlim/**
Facebook: **https://www.facebook.com/imartconsultant**

Closing Thoughts

Dear amazing reader,

I hope you enjoyed and were touched by these powerful chapters. Each author carefully handpicked stories from challenging times in their lives so they could inspire, educate, and empower you to realize your brilliance and to give you a sense of hope and encouragement, and let you know you are not alone.

We can't wait for you to break free to health and vitality and celebrate as you share your heartfelt love and compassion with the world.

I would like to share additional resources that will help you get unstuck and give you the tools that may support you as you build your lifelong wellness and optimal health.

I offer several workshops, group programs, and personal coaching.

1. **My first anthology, *The Authorities*, with *New York Times* bestselling author, Dr. John Gray, from the *Mars/Venus* series**. My chapter is called "Break Free from Your Pain Cycle," in which I *chronicle my transformation from being bedridden and in chronic pain to becoming a successful entrepreneur. I share the exact steps that I took that you could adopt for yourself. It's available on Amazon:* https://amzn.to/2H5LHmU

2. **Book Writing Opportunity**

Writing a book is an amazing way to share your expertise, knowledge and experiences. It gives an opportunity for your clients, prospects and your network to get to know you and build your influence.

It is also an incredible way to Increase Your **Visibility** where you are seen as an **Expert**, **Expand Your Influence** and **Make a Global Impact as a Published Author**!

Whether you are an established author or aspiring writer, our programs will support you. It is our goal to take the pressure off of the entire publishing work for you to become a published author so that you can focus on your writing to reach the readers who are yearning to hear your informative and life-changing message, and to boost your visibility, influence and success.

We are providing a platform for the everyday heroes in our backyards to share their amazing stories and become known, seen and heard. Yes! You too can be a published author! Usually, the first thought that comes in everybody's mind is that, "I don't have a story." Believe us, you do! We all have a story; to find yours, you can schedule a complimentary discovery call here: http://bit.ly/TalkwithSeema

3. **Reboot Program**

A sixteen-week program for women entrepreneurs and leaders to learn how they can eat, move, and think differently to ultimately create a life by your design, no longer by default.

You will learn:

- Four pillars to a healthier lifestyle
- How to make better life choices
- How to reclaim your body, mind, and spirit to live in the flow of your passion by building a strong wellness foundation.

4. ***Break Free to Brilliance* Podcast.**

Tune in to hear heart-centered guests for inspiration and insight as they share their experiences on how they broke free from their life challenges to live their purpose-driven life. These are the everyday heroes that you find in your backyard—mothers, sisters, friends, entrepreneurs, and business owners. We bring positive and transformational messages to the world so that we can make a lasting difference and help individuals powerfully live purposefully one show at a time.

5. We are continuously coming up with new, free resources to help you navigate how you want to move forward. You can find them at https://www.uplyft.media.

6. One of the key catalysts in turning my health around has been whole food supplements and the tower garden. You can find more information at www.seema.juiceplus.com or www.seemagiri.com.

If you are ready to shine and share your story of breaking free from challenges and living life on your terms, and if you are ready to help others stand in their power, you can participate in our upcoming anthologies and podcast.

If you would like to personally connect with me to explore opportunities in my programs, podcasts, and book-writing projects, then schedule a time with me at http://bit.ly/TalkwithSeema, or you can email me at seema@uplfyt.media.

May you always STAND IN YOUR POWER!

Sincerely,

Seema Giri

ACKNOWLEDGMENTS

It is beyond my wildest imagination to have this be the fourth book I have compiled. This has been a gift to me from the Universe, a divine intervention indeed. This can only happen when you have an amazing group of people that have your back.

I am grateful for my team of supporters to help bring forth my dream to help create a world where people live in peace and harmony. This is only possible when everyone is living in a state of health and vitality.

To my personal team, my husband, Upendra, and children, Aman and Ashima: You have shown immense love, trust and compassion. I love you for the way you always cheer me on and encourage me to embrace my brilliance.

Thanks to everyone on the publishing team for your amazing work to create this beautiful masterpiece.

I am grateful to the amazing group of collaborators, the co-authors who entrusted me to bring forward their powerful stories of breaking free to empowerment. Writing about the story of your life is a difficult and surreal process. Their stories are a work of deep reflection and storytelling, where they invite the readers into their world, describing their triumphs and disappointments that have shaped their lives to explore the opportunities to ultimately *The Art of Leadership: Leading Confidently in Any Season.*

Finally, I want to thank you, the reader, for leaning into these stories that will touch your heart and soul in profound ways. Allow yourself to embrace the gifts of love, wisdom and hope that will enrich your life's experience.

ABOUT THE AUTHOR

Seema Giri is an internationally bestselling and award-winning author, international speaker, empowerment leader, and multi-author book expert. Over the last twenty years, she has helped more than 100,000 spiritually aligned entrepreneurs and leaders expand their consciousness, tap into their inner power, and unleash their true potential so that they become unstoppable in business and life. Drawing from her own experiences with chronic illness, isolation, and deep feelings of emptiness and defeat, Seema offers insight and hope to leaders who want to shine.

After years of honing her craft and sharing her own story, her latest endeavor is to help others come out of the shadows by telling their own stories. She helps leaders and entrepreneurs expand their influence and impact through her *Shine Your Brilliance as an Author* program and storytelling platform. Her clients write high-impact books—sharing the wisdom they gained from life-altering experiences. As they do, the lives of readers are transformed, making a massive positive impact on the world.

Her expertise comes from a vast storehouse of experiences and opportunities, including traveling around the world. She draws from twenty years of project management, coaching, and leadership experience. She is an internationally bestselling and award-winning author, international speaker, and multi-author book expert. In addition to her own book projects and speaking engagements, she is proud to have co-authored the book *The Authorities*, with *New York Times* bestselling authors Dr. John Gray (*Men are from Mars, Women are from Venus*), Marci Shimoff (*Happiness for No Reason*), and Raymond Aaron (*Double Your Income Doing What You Love*). In it, she chronicles her transformation from being bedridden and in chronic pain to becoming a successful entrepreneur, mother, and wife. The rare combination of her personal testimony and her extensive expertise makes her a skilled and hopeful guide to all who want to tell their own stories and impact the world.

FB Page: Break Free to Stand in Your Power
https://www.facebook.com/seemagiri.standinyourpower/
Twitter: **https://twitter.com/giriseema**
Instagram: **https://www.instagram.com/giriseema1**
YouTube: Break Free to Brilliance **http://bit.ly/BreakFree2BrillianceChannel**
FB groups:
Self-Care to Profit for Women Entrepreneurs
https://www.facebook.com/groups/selfcartoprofit
Shine Your Brilliance as an Author
https://www.facebook.com/groups/shineyourbrilliance
LinkedIn: Seema Giri **www.linkedin.com/in/seema-giri-embracebrilliance**
Break Free to Brilliance Podcast **https://www.seemagiri.com/podcast/**
Website: **https://www.uplyft.media**
seema@uplfyt.media
mybestsellingbook@theuplyftmedia.com

"There are two primary choices in life: to accept conditions as they exist, or accept the responsibility for changing them."

—Dennis Waitley

What choices are you making?

Made in the USA
Middletown, DE
14 January 2022

58300760R00099